The WHITE BOY *and the* INDIANS

The WHITE BOY *and the* INDIANS

A MEMOIR OF RESERVATION LIFE, THE DEPRESSION, AND THE OKIES

PAUL AUSTIN JENNINGS

© 2022 by Paul Austin Jennings

All rights reserved. No part of this publication may be reproduced, stored in a retrieval system, or transmitted in any form or by any means—for example, electronic, photocopy, recording—without the prior written permission of the publisher. The only exception is brief quotations in printed reviews.

Library of Congress Control Number: 2022921011

ISBN 979-8-218-09256-6

Illustrations by Mercie Marshall at MercieMarshall.com

Interior design by Jerusha Agen

Photographs courtesy of the author

All Scripture quotations, unless otherwise indicated, are taken from the Holy Bible, New International Version®, NIV®. Copyright © 1973, 1978, 1984, 2011 by Biblica, Inc.™ Used by permission of Zondervan. All rights reserved worldwide. www.zondervan.com The "NIV" and "New International Version" are trademarks registered in the United States Patent and Trademark Office by Biblica, Inc.™

This book is lovingly dedicated to the memory of my mom and dad, Mary and Roy Jennings, who, because of their life of selfless giving to others, provided me with not just my experiences for these stories, but for the principles of living a God-honoring life for me and my siblings.

Contents

Preface xi
Introduction xiii
Geographical Section xv
Geographical Orientation xvii

Section One
A Simple Log Cabin Beginning
1. A Detached Garage and a Dugout Canoe 3
2. A Brand Spankin' New Home 9
3. A Big Projector and a Distinct Smell 15
4. Me and Thena and a Coiled Surprise 18

Section Two
Freight Trains & Ink Wells, Hobos & Okies
5. Our New Home in Denair 25
6. Readin', 'Ritin' and 'Rithmetic 28
7. Big Ink Day 37
8. A Lesson From the Okies 41
9. Movie Days 44
10. Kites 47
11. Myrna, the Saint, and Harry, the Scoundrel 50
12. Daily Vacation Bible School 60
13. Summer Days and Nights 64
14. Moses and Mom 69
15. Main Street 72
16. Frequent Freights and Hungry Hobos 81
17. Train Communication Problem 87

18. A Young Warrior's Weaponry and a Life Lesson 91
19. Free Haircut Anyone? 96
20. Swimming and Watermelons 99
21. Palatable Pleasantries and Peculiarities 104
22. Family Literary Lessons 109
23. Before TV and Social Media, There Was Radio 117

Section Three
Back to Indian Country

24. A Surprise Move 123
25. Martin's Ferry 126
26. Martin's Ferry Hotel 130
27. New School, New Friends 136
28. The Rise and Fall of Social Titans 141
29. Billy and Me and the Skunk 144
30. A Christmas Bear 150
31. John Luddington 155
32. A Day to Remember ... Or Forget 162
33. Scalping Woodpeckers 164
34. Special Saturday Adventures 168
35. My Pugilistic Beginnings and Endings 172
36. Eeling on the Mad River 175
37. Out of the Past 179
38. Closing Thoughts 186

Acknowledgments 191
Notes 193
About Paul Austin Jennings 195

Preface

A Surprising Start to This Special Story

In 1921, two well-educated and experienced Presbyterian church leaders from southern California—one an Army veteran, former boxer, pastor and scientist, the other a professor at a local Christian college—piled into a sleek Model T Ford and headed for a remote mountainous section of Humboldt County, some 700 miles to the north.

There was also a guy in the back seat. His dubious qualifications were being raised on a hardscrabble farm in Missouri, and he later worked as a hand on a cattle ranch in Rifle, Colorado. His education? He probably had completed no more than the seventh grade because of his work commitments on the family farm.

Even today, I can't explain how my dad, the guy in the back seat, met and developed a close friendship with the two churchmen. "Just a coincidence" doesn't seem to fit. Divine intervention does.

But here they were, this unlikely trio, on their way to check on and encourage a small Christian outpost on the

Hoopa Indian Reservation along the Trinity River, with the possibility of expanding the work to the Yurok and Karuk Indian tribes living nearby on the Klamath River.

One can only imagine the challenges of a road trip back then—the scarcity of motels (motor courts), restaurants and service stations, driving on dirt roads and plank roads and dodging other travelers with horse-drawn buggies or wagons. These men even went to areas where there were no roads, going on foot or on horseback to reach more isolated communities of Indians.

My parents' 1922 wedding photo

That trip outlined the course of history for my family for the next 15 years, and the influence on my life beyond that will be evidenced in many of the stories I'm sharing with you.

Dad was totally captivated by the missionary concept of being a friend with the Indians and sharing with them the truth of Christ's love.

Just one year after that road trip, my folks, newly married, began their work with the Hupas, and eventually with the two additional tribes.

In the process, they raised five kids, each of whom experienced primitive living and some of the Indian culture, such as enjoying the snug comforts of an Indian papoose basket in the early months of their lives.

This is my story....

Introduction

Because I'm 92 years old, my growing up years were of course far different than those of kids today. But what makes it even more unique was that I spent several of those years living in Indian country in northern California.

My first memory of a home was of a large one-room log cabin built by a Yurok Indian, and to get to it, we had to park on one side of the river and have Indian lads canoe us and our belongings and groceries and everything else over to the home.

In my seventh grade year, as the only white boy in a one-room Indian school, learning how to skin a skunk (very carefully) and why to scalp a woodpecker (to earn 10 cents a scalp), I thrived on having a real pioneer living experience.

I also lived in the small railroad town of Denair in the Central Valley of California during the Depression years. In my elementary school lunchroom, I watched in utter amazement as my eighth grade "Okie" classmate made sandwiches for his younger siblings, using lard from a bucket he brought from home and a loaf of bread he bought each morning on his way to school.

In the classroom, the pungent odors came from the shoes of kids who had to milk cows before school. On the playground, we played Mumbley Peg with our pocketknives, and on Kite Day, we marveled at the beautiful and intricately made kites flown by the Japanese kids and their families, the same families who later were hustled off to internment camps.

These stories will give you a first-hand look at our lives and times, when we stood and saluted the flag every morning and often sang a verse or two of "My Country 'Tis of Thee."

The tales I tell, most historical and some hysterical, are all presented in truth and love to kids everywhere and of every age. I hope you will enjoy them and gain more of an understanding of how life used to be for a boy growing up in the 1930s and '40s.

Geographical Section

Map of Humboldt County

Geographical Orientation

HUMBOLDT COUNTY

Where a lot of the action takes place

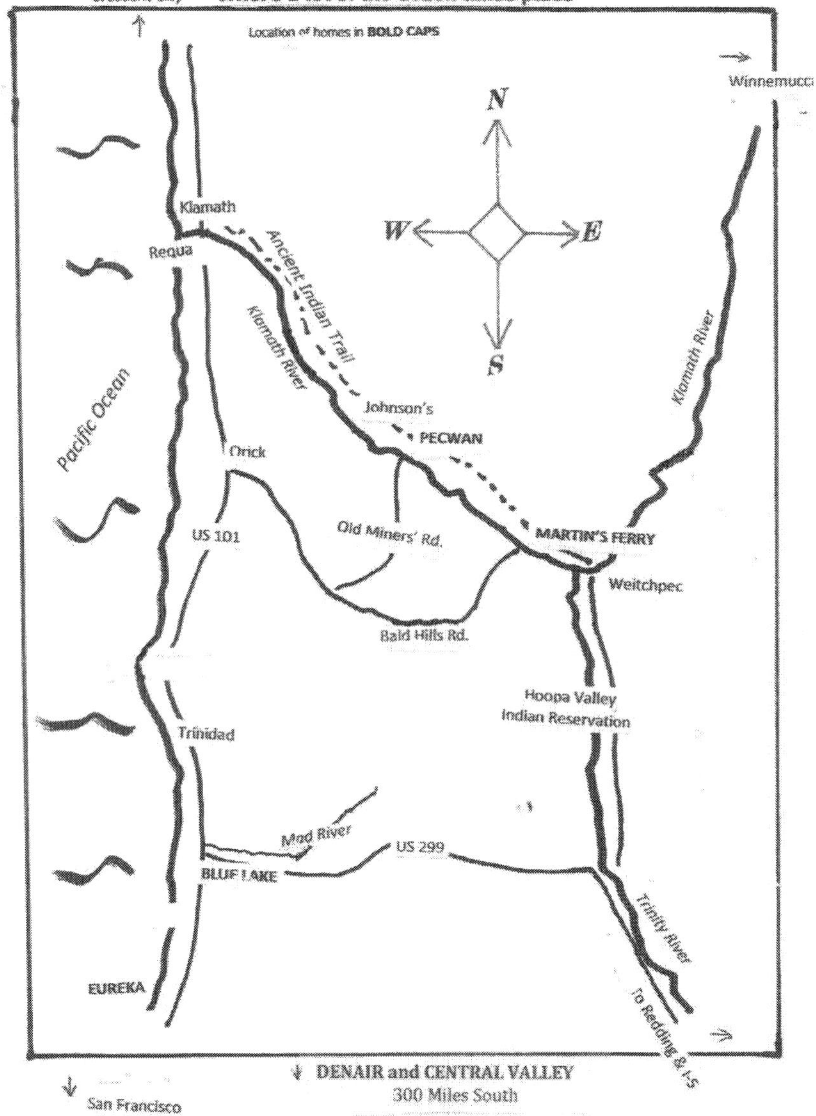

Geographical Orientation

You Can't Tell the Players without a Program

Because my family made several significant moves during my early years, and my stories follow these moves, this geographical and chronological orientation and the accompanying map will help you follow the flow of those moves and related stories.

The locations referred to are Pecwan, Weitchpec, Denair, Martin's Ferry and Blue Lake, little known to the outside world, but key places in my early life. They can be found along the Klamath River in Humboldt County and along the Santa Fe Railroad in California's Central Valley.

Humboldt County lies in the northwest sector of California with only 90 miles of Del Norte County separating it from Oregon. The main towns in the county are Garberville and, 75 miles to the north, the larger coastal towns of Eureka and Arcata.

The part of Humboldt County that is the focus of many of the stories in this book is the Klamath River/Trinity River section that lies between Highway

101, the Redwood Highway, to the west, and US-99 and I-5 to the east. The area in between is mostly mountainous—the Coast Range, Trinity Alps and Marble Mountains (great fishing). The Trinity River (more good fishing) flows through the Hoopa Indian Reservation and into the Klamath River (the state's second largest river) at Weitchpec.

Note that the Klamath River (legendary steelhead and salmon fishing) coming down from its headwaters in Oregon makes a big right turn at Weitchpec and flows northwest past Martin's Ferry, past Pecwan and empties into the Pacific Ocean near the town of Klamath on US-101. Now would be a good time to check the map.

The stories that follow are in three sections, each based on a particular time and location of our family home.

Section 1 deals with the first five years of my life. Born in the Indian Hospital on the Hoopa Indian Reservation in 1930, my very first memories of life came while living in our Indian-built log cabin home in Pecwan on the lower Klamath River. We were five kids; I was number four. Mom taught school on the reservation and Dad was doing his Christian work with the Indians. We were living without electricity or indoor plumbing or even a road to the house. It made for a challenging and creative way to begin life.

We left Humboldt County in 1935, after Mom and Dad had completed 15 years of working with the Hupa, Karuk and Yurok tribes (Hupa was the name of the tribe; Hoopa was the name of the reservation). We moved to the small railroad town of Denair in the Central Valley of California, which is where Section 2 takes place.

Here I went to grades 1 through 6 during the Depression years, marked by widespread poverty, social unrest, and major immigration from the Midwest by folks escaping the prolonged and severe drought (the Dust Bowl).

This was John Steinbeck country, vividly described in his notable work, *The Grapes of Wrath*. Exciting times, but aren't the grammar school years momentous and formative years for most kids? And here in the valley we had electricity and running water.

Section 3 deals with our move back to Humboldt County, back to Indian country and the small community of Martin's Ferry. We were back to coal oil lamps and outhouses. As the only white boy in a one-room Indian school, I joined with my fellow seventh grader and Indian mentor Billy as I set out to learn the Indian and pioneer ways of life.

Each of these experiences, each distinctly different, presented their own successes and failures. I invite you to come on a unique adventure: Explore with me, laugh with me, cry with me and join me in an unforgettable trip through times and places likely unfamiliar to most of you.

Let's get started....

Section One

A Simple Log Cabin Beginning

Humboldt County, Klamath River

1930-1933: "Bob's Old Place," Martin's Ferry

1934-1935: Log Cabin, Pecwan, 17 miles downriver from Martin's Ferry

Chapter 1

A Detached Garage and a Dugout Canoe

Few things capture our early memories more than the homes in which we lived, the location, the weather, and the construction or other special items tickling our minds, bringing pleasure or pathos.

For me, my three homes in the Indian country of the Klamath Mountains of Northern California hold an amazing variety of recollections that I still cherish after more than four score years.

The first home on this short list is what my family affectionately called "Bob's Old Place" in Martin's Ferry. It belonged to the Roberts family, of which Bob was the patriarch, and it was already old when we lived there.

Bob Roberts was an elderly leader of the Yuroks in this area; dad had met him on his first visit to Indian country, and our families maintained a close relationship with the Roberts family over the years. Bob had been known by the natives as "Waseck Bob," identifying the Indian name for that area.

I don't remember living there, as we moved to

Pecwan when I was three years old. But subsequent nostalgic visits by me and various family members to the long-vacant old homesite revealed several factors attesting to its antiquity.

Newspapers put up *after* we had moved were covering the walls of the small house and provided some very out-of-date but fun reading experiences: "Jesse Owens won four gold medals at the Olympics (1936)" and "More dust storms are causing people to leave the Midwest (late 1930s) and "if we would hustle over to Brizzard's store, we could get a 5-pound bag of flour for 25 cents and a dozen eggs for 40 cents."

While scrounging around the building, my kids extracted several *square nails* from some of the old timbers. This really was Bob's *old* place. A few years later on our next visit, we were saddened to see the house had finally collapsed and was partly covered by wild berry vines. Eventually, those vines, scrub brush, pepperwood trees and a few conifers took over completely and obscured every evidence of human habitation.

My second home with more of an impact on my life was our log cabin near Pecwan on the lower Klamath River, a community of 20 or 25 Indian families where I lived as a 4- and 5-year-old. The remote location is one of the primary characteristics of this home. I mean really remote, as in you couldn't get there by car because there was no road to the place.

This left walking or riding a horse 15 miles over the trail from Martin's Ferry, where the road from Hoopa ended, to our log cabin. That ancient trail continued all the way downriver to the old Indian community of Requa (near Klamath) where the river emptied into the ocean. For hundreds of years, that had been the primary trade route between the coastal Yurok Indians and those living up and down the river.

One other option remained, which as it turned out, provided the best solution, and it's a dilly. You need to hear this, and I will get back to the cabin story in a minute.

We had a detached garage. It was detached from the cabin by about 100 yards, 30 of which was the mighty Klamath River, the third largest river on the Pacific Coast. There was a road from the "outside" down to the river across from our cabin. It was probably put in by the mining companies some 40 or 50 years before we came on the scene, but their operations had long since abandoned this area.

The maintenance of the road was left to the elements and the few people who occasionally used it, like my dad. It was not hard to understand why Dad always carried a shovel, an ax and a saw because winter landslides, deep ruts and fallen trees were common and frequent obstacles.

It was there on the west bank of the river that our detached garage, a small open-sided shed providing a meager cover for our 1928 Erskine, was located. (Check the map for the road leading from the Bald Hills Road down to Pecwan.) So we had a garage and we had a car that was capable of getting supplies from stores in town, but all of this was across the river from our home.

Taking the trail from the log cabin down to the river was simple enough, as was walking up the opposite bank to the garage. That watery section in the middle did pose a problem. There was no bridge or zip line, but we had good neighbors. Dad had negotiated the services of two stalwart local Indian boys and their family's dugout canoe to do the honors of ferrying him back and forth across the river.

This worked out quite well as long as we could find the boys and the river wasn't too high and turbulent from recent rains. This idea of a plan "working out quite well" is relative, considering the alternative of the horseback trail.

Here is the route Dad would take to get to the closest store for groceries and supplies, assuming the canoe crew had been found and had transported him from the cabin across the river to the car: The first leg of the journey would be up this primitive road from the banks of the river to the Bald Hills Road.

Next there was a little jaunt of 35 twisting miles to the town of Orick on Highway 101, then south another 25 miles to Arcata and Brizzards store, then back again, usually an all-day venture.

At times, he didn't get home until after dark. I recall us kids anxiously waiting to see the car's headlights appear and disappear over the last twisting mile completing the trip, and then we heard the car's horn, which was a signal to the canoe paddlers that their services were needed again. Dad was home, probably with some fresh apples or oranges, and maybe some candy.

My parents in working clothes, 1924

The good news is that while we lived in Pecwan, the road was completed on our side of the river to and past our cabin another mile to the Pecwan school, and one more mile on down to the community of Johnsons, which was as far as the road would ever go. The need for the canoe river crossing was no more, and our car found a home near our log cabin.

Details of my third unique home in Humboldt

County will be found in Section 3. On a cultural note, the Yurok dugout canoes, each individually carved from a redwood log, were once the main mode of transportation between the people of the Hupa, Yurok and Karuk tribes.

They are still a vital element of some of their ancient ceremonies, such as the White Deerskin Dance. With the Yurok people, the redwood canoe was more than a vessel of transportation, as they are considered spiritual beings integral to their creation stories. Carved into the bottom of each canoe is a heart, lungs and kidneys.

Now, about that log cabin ...

Chapter 2

A Brand Spankin' New Home

I wish I knew how and when my dad made arrangements with Charlie Myers for our family to move into his just-barely-completed log cabin.

My brother Ben with our log cabin, 1934

You can see in the picture that there wasn't a front porch or even steps to the front door when we moved in (steps were added later), and the area around the house wasn't cleaned up or leveled. That's my brother, Ben, in the picture. He was a seventh grader when we moved in.

Charlie Myers was a local Yurok Indian and obviously a very capable craftsman, including the related skills of site development, architecture, logger (felling and hauling trees) roofer, specializing in cedar shake roofs, and finish carpentry. Well, actually not much of that. There was no need for building inspections of the electricity or plumbing or insulation, because there was none.

I can only assume Charlie did some clearing of the area for the cabin. There may have been a slight clearing there to begin with. Maybe he whacked down a few trees, pulled out an old stump or two and blasted some inconvenient rocks; I just don't know.

But here's what I do know: He located some 30 or 40 trees of the right size, about a foot in diameter, felled the trees, and towed them to the building site, using a horse to bring them in one at a time. He then removed the limbs and bark of each log, cut it to the right length to allow for doors and windows, and notched the logs for the corners of the building. For the floor, Charlie sawed heavy planks and then found cedar logs that he split for the shakes on the roof and the front of the house.

The year-round spring, about 25 feet from the house, would have been one of the primary reasons Charlie built the cabin on this particular piece of land.

Assembling all of this likely required some extra help, maybe a neighbor or his wife, Melissa. As for the tools he used, you can imagine there were several axes, a couple of hammers, a six-foot crosscut saw, a draw knife, adze, sledgehammer and a couple of steel wedges. To make sure things lined up, Charlie probably had a square, a tape measure, a level and plumb line, and a whole lot of elbow grease. One story is that Charlie laid out 65 cents for some nails, his total cash expenditure.

The result of Charlie Myers' extraordinary effort was a spacious 20-foot by 30-foot one-room snug cabin (I don't remember chilly drafts between the logs or any leaks from the shake roof). There was a front door and a side door and two openings for windows on one side of the house, which were filled not with glass windowpanes, but heavy oil paper, which let in some light and kept out some cold. There were no interior walls, so my folks hung some blankets or curtains in one corner to create a sense of privacy for their "bedroom."

The bedroom for us five kids was the rest of the house, which also served as the kitchen, dining room and living room, but no bathroom. However, our amazing builder had thought of everything. While we had chamber pots for immediate use, Charlie had built a very serviceable "one-holer" outhouse, for which we were thankful.

We had two stoves in the cabin, and I don't think these came across the river in the dugout canoe. They came over the trail on the sturdy backs of a horse or mule. I recall the big kitchen stove near one corner of the room and the smaller potbelly stove near the center. A teakettle was usually on the small stove, providing moisture for the room and hot water for dad's coffee and our chocolate or tea. We had found some tea plants conveniently growing near our spring.

Several irons for ironing clothes rested on one corner

of the kitchen stove. These were the kind of irons that had a removable handle so that as an iron cooled while ironing clothes, it could be placed back on the stove and the handle used to pick up another iron that had been heating.

The wood box beside the stove required constant refilling from the ricks of wood outside, and my brothers and I were assigned the responsibility of making sure that box was never empty. Even as a five-year-old, I was expected to be part of that essential chore, even if I carried only one stick at a time. A rick of wood, by the way, is a stack that measures eight feet long and four feet high, and our stoves took 16-inch pieces of wood, so that three ricks would make up one cord of wood.

We had washtubs—inside for personal hygiene and outside over a wood fire for washing clothes. Wait just a minute—you're probably thinking that washtub stuff went out with the covered wagons or Little House on the Prairie or a Clint Eastwood movie, but not so.

When the water in the outside tub was hot, Mom applied the soap and proceeded to scrub the clothes on the washboard. Washboards really did have a use other than as a percussion instrument in a hillbilly band. The clothes were then pinned to the clothesline, which was strung between the house and one of the nearby trees.

We had running water. Not in pipes; someone had to run to the spring with a jar or a bucket to bring water into the house. Indoor lighting was provided by kerosene lanterns, both the kind with a cloth wick that could be adjusted with a little knob on the side to regulate the amount of light, and the lantern that used a silk wick, which provided even better light.

After living in the log cabin for two years, we moved when I was 5 to the Central Valley of California.

When we visited Pecwan about five years later, the cabin had taken on a new look: Two windows and a porch had been added to the front, and real glass replaced the oil paper windows.

Me, Bette, and Mom (front row) at the renovated cabin, 1938

There are many life lessons we all learned from living so close together and as members of a minority group, although I don't think we ever thought of that. One lesson is the love we felt for each other. How grateful I am for the family and spiritual bonds that bound us.

Another strand woven into our fabric is our acceptance and love for folks different from us, and particularly the Indian people we lived with. Dad was the prime example of that attitude, but it has been manifested by the rest of us in many ways. Several of us maintained contact with some of the Indian families over many years.

Seven people living in a 20-foot by 30-foot one-room log cabin can test the mettle in the best of folks. For my family, it brought out the best in us.

Unfortunately, the Klamath River flood of 1958 took out the log cabin. Gone, but never forgotten.

Chapter 3

A Big Projector and a Distinct Smell

Much of Dad's work with the Indians was just that, "work with the Indians," as in helping repair a fence or clearing brush or preparing a patch of ground for a garden. These were times of getting acquainted, establishing trust and demonstrating the care and love he had for these people.

One of Dad's successful tools for a more formal gathering was a slide projector, a Stereopticon lantern, that he used to illustrate his talks. Two things stand out in my memory about the procedure involved when the projector was used: the size of the projector and the smell. The large size is easy to understand because of the bulk of any of the older projectors. The smell is definitely unique because the light used to project the images came from burning carbide gas, and burning carbide has a distinctive odor.

I remember Dad placing a small amount of carbide crystals in a container and hooking it to a small can of water. Water dripping into the carbide crystals produced a gas that was forced through a small jet and lit with a match or flint. The flame and the amount of light it produced were controlled by the rate of the water dripping onto the carbide crystals. That gas came equipped with its own distinct odor that we all accepted as just part of a pleasant experience.

Pictures were projected on the wall of a room using 3-inch-by-3-inch glass slides. Dad had a number of sets of slides illustrating several biblical stories, but he usually started the program with a short series of comical slides, which the Indians enjoyed immensely. One of the introductory sets of slides depicted some cartoon drawings of ducks going through a variety of humorous antics. At the bottom of each slide was a brief narrative describing the action, and each set of slides ended with a moral teaching. Few of the older Indians could read, so Dad read the story as he went through the slides. These were the only times I remember Dad using his rich baritone voice to follow a comedy routine.

The Bible story slides were then used as Dad told the more meaningful lessons from the Word.

At the end of the lesson, the water dripping into the carbide was turned off and the flame gradually went out. The old carbide-burning Stereopticon lantern had proven its worth once again. Then after the room darkening curtains were taken down from the windows as the carbide smell was diminishing, we sang one verse of a hymn and Dad gave a brief benediction.

The final and also productive event was enjoying

Mom's room temperature Kool-Aid (hey, there was no ice) and usually some cookies brought by one of the Indian ladies. The Indians were generally a jovial bunch of people and it was fun being around them during these informal times ... and I really enjoyed the cookies!

Chapter 4

Me and Thena and a Coiled Surprise

I was mesmerized by the sight of the coiled snake in front of me. The tiny unblinking black eyes staring back at me, the tongue flicking in and out and the soft sound of the shaking rattles at the end of the tail captured my attention.

I'd had brief glimpses of snakes before they slithered away into the grass or bushes. This guy wasn't going away, just sitting there like maybe he wanted to be a friend. Thena needed to see this. "Thena, come look. There's a thnake thticking hith tongue out at me."

Thena Thompson, my young Yurok babysitter, had been quietly soaking up the morning sun with a watchful eye on me as I played in the front yard of our log cabin. (The rest of the family, two brothers and two sisters, were away at school a mile down the road where Mom was one of two teachers in the Pecwan school.)

My unusual and excited request snapped Thena to attention. She hustled to check the validity of my claim, no doubt wondering what this little guy was up to.

Thena took one look at the tense situation, and like the calm before the storm, she paused for a whole half second, and then like a tornado she struck in a blur of action. First she quickly snatched me up and unceremoniously dumped me about 10 feet away. Away from the threatening coiled Pacific Rattlesnake.

I don't recall anything Thena said. What I do remember was a sudden and dramatic change in Thena from the usually calm and loving young woman to a driven, determined attacker.

She grabbed a garden hoe that had been leaning up against the cabin and went for the snake, which had started to crawl away.

But escape was not in the cards for this snake on this day.

Her yelling and screaming was scary to me as she frantically but effectively chopped at the snake until there was no more movement.

Still scared and confused by the wild scene I had just witnessed, I felt better when she finally stopped and stood silently, breathing heavily, just staring at the bloody remains of the snake.

Shortly after the frightening drama, Thena took my hand and led me to the steps of the log cabin, where we sat as she caught her breath.

I'm sure we discussed the dangers of rattlesnakes and the need to avoid them when possible, and that I should be careful when playing outside.

But my actual memory is of her holding me close for a long time and sobbing softly.

Later that afternoon after the family had returned home from school, Thena slowly—almost reluctantly, as if she would rather not even think about it—told the story of the morning's momentous episode.

In wide-eyed amazement, my siblings watched and listened as she related the details.

"Thena killed the rattlesnake. There is still blood on the hoe. And look at that mess that was once a rattlesnake. Wow! She saved our little brother from its poisonous fangs. Didn't know Thena could do that."

But she could and she did.

My mom, with tears in her eyes, and Dad could hardly express enough of their heartfelt thanks for the brave heroics of this normally quiet Indian girl.

After my dad had buried the mangled remains of the snake, he attempted to give Thena the eight-segmented rattle he had removed from the snake's tail. She wanted nothing to do with it.

As the story has been retold, it seems that the rattlesnake was eight feet long, had a girth of 12 inches and had recently devoured two squirrels, a rabid porcupine, a small goat and was about to have a little boy for dessert. There's always been some question concerning the veracity of twice-told tales.

But for one young courageous babysitter and one adventuresome little boy, the story without any embellishments is real enough as first told.

One historical note: According to early census records, produced for me by my friend Helen Roberts, Thena Thompson was the granddaughter of author Lucy Thompson (1856-1932), who was from Pecwan and known for her book, *To the American Indian, The Unique Personal Account of the Yurok Native American Woman of Northern California.*

Section Two

Freight Trains & Ink Wells, Hobos & Okies

Denair, Central Valley of California

1936-1941: My elementary years, grades 1-6

Chapter 5

Our New Home in Denair

Or Where Is the Outhouse?

I don't know exactly how it happened, but one morning we loaded up the car and drove to Denair (I had never heard of it), a small farming town in Central California. We had left behind our snug, one-room log cabin in Pecwan and the Indian families who would come by to visit. The mountains were exchanged for absolutely flat country.

We arrived at a completely different kind of house—one with several rooms and a toilet that flushed and sinks with water from faucets. There were a lot of people that I didn't know around us, and there were no Indians.

That was a load of changes for this 6-year-old to understand. In the summer of 1936, after my folks' 15 years of ministering to the Indians in northern California, they decided to close that chapter of their lives and move with their five kids to the Central Valley of California. I don't know why. Maybe they were plain worn out physically and emotionally from the pretty grim life we had been living, although they knew about those conditions when they started the work.

More likely, they wanted a more complete educational and social experience for us kids. Ben and Mary were approaching high school age and stood a better chance of developing their potential in a more traditional setting.

They chose Denair because of the Missionary Church there. My mom and her large family had deep roots in the large parent Missionary Church in Van Nuys, California, but living in the Central Valley was more appealing than living in the Los Angeles area. So with the church as our anchor, we settled in Denair.

My dad painted houses for a local contractor, although there were not always houses to paint, and my mom taught elementary school, which provided a more reliable income in these Depression years. My older siblings usually had part-time jobs, but life for us younger kids was simple and mostly enjoyable.

My adjustment to this new life did not come without a few bumps. I had never before had indoor plumbing and looked around for the comfort of an outhouse. I also was longing for the metal bucket and dipper to get a cool drink.

And there were so many people around! Just a couple of days after our arrival, we went to church and there must've been 50 people in that big room, and they all started singing songs. It was noisy. I was used to a dozen or so Indians when my dad held a service. Then there was an announcement that the kids would be going to their classes.

I was mighty glad that the day before our family had gotten together with the Doerksens because their son, Art, was my age. I badly needed a friend in this strange place. He told me to follow him, and I tagged along until we got to the head of a long stairway leading down underground. This did not look good to me—I had never been in a basement before—but I grabbed onto Art's shirt while he led me downstairs to our classroom.

I grew to like that basement classroom because it was quieter than up above, with only half a dozen or so kids my age. There was also a great big furnace and a coal bin for heating the church in the winter. And there was real black shiny coal in the bin.

Then there were local stores in town, which was an amazing concept. No more daylong trips for dad to get supplies or canoe trips to get them back home. Now it was a simple five-minute walk from our home to a store in town.

I remember thinking, "Someday I'm going to get some money and walk right into that store and buy some stuff." I eventually did that. And I learned that basements are safe and that indoor plumbing is a pretty good thing after all.

I still had a lot to learn....

Chapter 6

Readin', 'Ritin' and 'Rithmetic

My grammar school years were filled with a variety of highlights and hijinks, as I'm guessing most of yours were, too. Those were formative and informative times for most of us. We learned to read and write, and we learned to make friends and we learned that some of our actions were acceptable and some were not.

You will see that some of my experiences were very similar to yours, but a bunch of them, because I was in a pre-Internet and even a pre-television world, will be strangely different. So hang on while we take a look at my classrooms in the mid-1930s to mid-1940s.

My first school experience in the first grade was particularly daunting. We had just moved from the Indian reservation where I had little chance of being with groups of kids my own age. I'd gotten to know Art a couple of weeks earlier, and he served as my early guide and mentor.

It is interesting to note that my first grade classroom

was the Little Red Schoolhouse. No joke; a little red schoolhouse. It was old, it had only one room and it was painted red, having served for many years as the only school in town. It was now affectionately called the Little Red Schoolhouse.

Just a couple of years after I moved on, it gave way to a city park. The permanent elementary school was a couple of blocks away, built of red bricks and considered the "new school."

Several features were common in every classroom. Portraits of George Washington and Abraham Lincoln, as well as the American flag were prominently displayed at the front of the room. The flag was saluted every morning, led by that week's flag monitor who gave the commands, "Stand, ready, salute." We stood, placed our right hand over our hearts and gave our pledge.

Several of my classrooms had cloakrooms, a partitioned section in the back of the room that was good for a little morning chitchat with our friends before school got started. A row of coat hooks on one side of the room and a shelf on the other side served the real purpose of the cloakroom: Hanging up jackets and sweaters and setting aside our lunch pails or brown bags until lunchtime.

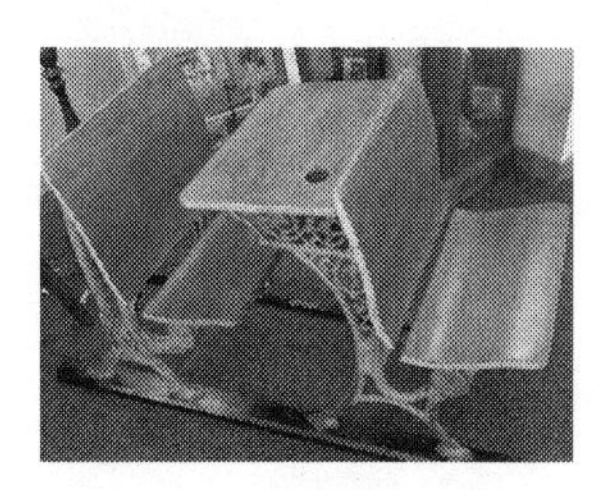

The wrought iron desks with the flip-up seat and the desktop with a hole for the inkwell were attached to runners and aligned in five or six rows. Some of the wooden desktops had been resurfaced over the summer in an attempt to remove the initials and other creative carvings by former students.

Often on the first morning, we could choose our own seating section, but usually by the second or third day the teacher would wisely have developed a seating chart that provided the most successful classroom decorum. I wonder if that explains why Art and I, in the fifth grade, were never seated close to each other.

On the front wall of the classroom and behind the teacher's desk were the blackboards (actually more green than black), the focal point of a lot of the classroom activities. There were also one or two blackboards on the side of the room. Alphabet charts showing both print and cursive letters were above the chalkboards in every classroom.

The teachers used the blackboards for listing lesson assignments, special notices of upcoming events, or often illustrating a new concept in math or writing. One corner of the board was reserved for writing down the names of students who had somehow crossed the line of acceptable behavior, usually too much talking or not raising a hand before speaking or chewing gum and the like. These special kids might lose a recess or have a note sent home to their folks.

I believe it was in the fourth grade that Miss Gilvere used the front board to introduce long division. We learned about the dividend, the divisor, the quotient and the remainder, and practiced our new process endlessly on the boards where the teacher could easily see and correct our mistakes.

Learning the times table up to 12 times 12 was also a

big part of our program. We used flashcards to practice. We had contests, one row against another or boys against girls, to show off our efficiency in, or lack of, knowing the times tables.

After any vacation, we knew we were going to have to write about our activities in our time off from school. This was a good writing exercise, but the real fun came when we read our stories to the whole class. That exposed the level of our writing skill, but also exposed a lot about our lives and our families.

These activities took a lot of board space for practice and used up a lot of chalk, plus created a surplus of chalk dust, which gave rise to the need for blackboard monitors. Two students were selected to serve as blackboard monitors for a week at a time.

Briefly, their duties were to collect the blackboard erasers at the end of every day, take them outside and bang them together to get rid of the accumulated chalk dust. The monitors also cleaned the chalk dust out of the chalk tray at the bottom of each blackboard so that every day started with relatively clean chalkboards and erasers.

Clear in my memory is an incident that occurred one day while Art and I were working at the chalkboard "practicing our spelling words." He leaned over to my side of the board, and above the words we were writing, he drew a stick figure of a boy with a dotted line coming down from between his legs. Before my eraser could eliminate this rude intrusion into my space, the ever-watchful eye of my teacher, Miss Gilvere, took in the scene. "Arthur and Paul, take your seats immediately."

This was not the first time our names had been linked

in a stern voice. But the evidence was clear, and whether it was fear of the teacher or loyalty to a buddy, the real story never came out officially, and Art and I spent several recesses inside as punishment, while I reminded him of what a scoundrel he was.

Each of my classrooms from the middle of elementary school on up had a collection of pull-down maps attached to the top of the blackboard in the front of the room. These maps were usually based on the curriculum of that particular grade, but there also were maps of the world, the United States, North America and South America.

These maps undoubtedly contributed to my enjoyment of maps and geography for the rest of my life. We would have drills where the student would go to the map and point out capitals of states and countries. Or we located mountain ranges and major rivers and seaports.

We learned about the Andes and the Appalachians. About Chile and Santiago, New Mexico and Santa Fe, and the Mississippi and Missouri and the Klamath rivers. And then, using the old spinning globe, also in every classroom, we searched to see who could first find Madagascar or the Solomon Islands.

Most families did little travel outside of our country or even outside our state, so all of the work that we did with the maps in our classroom proved a necessary link to our grasp of geography.

Writing instruction and related techniques had a life of its own. First graders were issued a fat green pencil with no eraser. When the pencil had to be sharpened, the dial on the front of the pencil sharpener had to be rotated to a larger size to accommodate the fat green pencil.

Often a student from the fifth or sixth grade would volunteer to go to the first grade classroom to sharpen the fat green pencils for the next day. From the second grade on, the yellow pencil with an eraser was commonly used. We got a new one each month, as I recall, which seemed adequate for most of the girls, but for some of us guys, that pencil too often became a 2-inch stub long before the end of the month.

One of the more serious concerns was that the knowledgeable educators of that time, probably people from the county office of education, insisted that the middle graders learn how to write with a pen and ink. Small matter, you say? Not so. Remember this salient fact: Mr. Fountain and Mr. Ball had not yet created their pens for classroom use.

The poor precursor to those instruments was a penholder, a metal pen point and an inkwell to complete the challenging task of writing with ink. If you, the reader, were not subjected to this exercise in your early schooling, be very thankful. Because of the drama and trauma that the first day of ink writing held for many of us, I'm addressing this issue in the next story, "Big Ink Day."

In learning to read, I just missed out on Noah Webster's *Blue-Backed Speller*, which had been used for 150 years, and McGuffey Readers, each of which sold over 100 million copies. These readers were phonetically based and strongly presented Christian principles.

Other books that were widely used when our country

was young were the *New England Primer*, *Webster's Dictionary of the English Language*, and the Bible. The literacy rate in parts of New England was more than 90 percent. I was introduced to the new "whole word" method of reading with the "Dick and Jane" series. Instead of having "In Adam's fall we sinned all" as an initial learning experience, I remember this stirring tale: "What can Father see? What can Mother see? What can Dick and Jane see? Baby said, 'See, see.'"

Fortunately we all learned to read over the next several years and most of us discovered the enjoyment and excitement of reading. For me, the writing of Mark Twain, Howard Pease, Jack London and others thrilled me, as I discovered amazing people and places I would never find in our little town.

One element that was critical in our lives as school kids was the innocence we had about life and how naïve we were about growing up. Every classroom had a dictionary, and in the middle grades, there was an encyclopedia. These sources, along with talking with our parents and schoolyard chatter provided us with basic information about life and the world. There were times when this limited kind of information was woefully inadequate.

Here's a quirky example of that innocence, that naiveté that characterized my life back then. In the fourth grade, several of us boys were given an astounding bit of anatomical knowledge. I think Donnie brought it to school one day that girls had a spleen, and that spleen had to do with the very private part of her body that was related to sex. (Remember, we had no Internet.) And we boys, having acquired this most secretive bit of information, took it upon ourselves to demonstrate our manly knowledge with the girls.

During the next recess that day, we whispered loudly among ourselves, making sure that girls nearby could hear us, such witty comments as, "Did you know that girls have a spleen?" Snicker, snicker. This obviously led to embarrassments and indignation by the girls who made sure that Miss Gilvere heard about it.

When we came in from the recess the day we had launched our campaign of enlightenment, Miss Gilvere, her face clouded in anger, tore into us. "You boys," and I know there were some descriptive adjectives that she would have liked to have thrown in, but she didn't. "You boys think you are so smart, but you were so wrong and so rude to be talking to the girls about a spleen."

Oh my gosh, she had said "spleen!"

And then she made this arresting statement: "Everybody has a spleen and it has nothing to do with what you are thinking. Each of you boys has a spleen."

What? Everybody has a spleen? Art and Jimmy and I had spleens? Where did Donnie get...? And right then and there the ignorant wind was gone from our now tattered sails. We had been had. An embarrassing lesson learned the hard way.

World War II became increasingly important to us kids in my upper elementary years. We felt we were in the know with our early drawings of Hitler and Mussolini, small mustache and hair combed over his forehead for the German chancellor, and the big jaw with a cigarette in a long cigarette holder for the Italian dictator.

Our fantasies soon gave way to reality as we heard on

the evening news about the German bombing of London and our own planes bombing Germany. It was hard to comprehend how so many lives, first hundreds and then thousands, could be lost so suddenly. We became familiar with our country's warplanes, the B-17 Flying Fortress, the B-24 Liberator, the P-38 Lightning and the P-51 Mustang fighter planes.

We learned about the Norden Bombsight, which according to the Army Air Force information office enabled pilots to "drop a bomb into a pickle barrel from 30,000 feet." It was a good instrument, but that description was way over the top. All this equipment was matched against the German Luftwaffe with their Stuka dive bombers and Messerschmitt fighters.

The war in the Pacific involved the B-25 Martin Bomber and the P-40 Warhawks. These were the Flying Tigers with the dramatic painting of shark's teeth in the front of the plane that fought with and for the Chinese, usually against the Japanese Zeros.

I remember in the seventh grade while living in Martin's Ferry (more about that time will come in Section 3), I whittled and put together a P-40 using redwood to form the fuselage and lighter colored cedar for the wings and tail. That little plane proudly lasted through all the war years and many years thereafter, until it was badly damaged, not by the Japanese Zeros, but by the family dog.

Elementary school years: Fun times, learning times, times of getting ready for the next chapter of our lives.

Chapter 7

Big Ink Day

This was "Big Ink Day," as declared by some of us very knowledgeable guys who knew what was coming. It was the day our inkwells got ink. The day we learned to write on ink paper with a pen and ink. The day we graduated from just pencil and arithmetic paper to write with real ink on real ink paper. Somebody, probably someone at the county schools office, decided that fourth graders needed to learn to write with ink. And this was that day.

Most of us knew a little bit about this advanced form of communication. We'd seen our moms or dads or older brothers or sisters writing with ink, and a lot of us had done a little scribbling with it ourselves.

Our teacher, Miss Gilvere, had told us the day before that this would be ink writing day and that when we arrived at school, there would be ink in our inkwells, the same inkwells that from the first day of school had remained quietly and dryly nestled in the hole in our desktop in the upper right-hand corner of the desk.

Now Big Ink Day had arrived. We came into the classroom, put our lunch pails and lunch bags on the shelf in the cloakroom, stood by our desks and, following the lead of our flag salute monitor, said the Pledge of Allegiance. No sooner had we chorused "with liberty and justice for all," when Miss Gilvere got our immediate attention with "Before you take your seats, I just want to remind you that there is ink in your inkwells." She might just as well have said, "There is nitroglycerin in your inkwells, and if you jostle your desk, just a little bit of it will explode." All of us got the message, even Leonard, a big awkward kid who usually dropped and flopped into his seat (he would have been the first to go kaboom). We gently eased into our seats.

To further impress us with the importance of this day, our teacher gave the details of her preparation. She explained that she and a couple of helpers from the upper grades, before school that morning, had collected all of the inkwells and put them on the table in the back of the room where they unscrewed the plastic tops.

One of the helpers with very steady hands poured about half an inch of ink into each inkwell using the special ink jar with a special ink-pouring spout. They had then replaced the cover on each inkwell and carefully took them back to our desks.

While this was being explained to the class, a question came up in the minds of a couple of us guys: What if our particular inkwell had not been filled and had somehow been missed? In order to check out the possibility of this gross omission being made, we needed something to probe the inkwell to determine the presence of ink. Our pencil was the most logical thing to use, so Art and I very quietly dipped our pencils into the inkwell, and sure enough, there was ink in there. Yep, now there was also ink on our pencils. We, quick thinkers that we were, quickly solved the problem by wiping the pencils on the cuff of our pants. All was well.

The momentous lesson began with the paper monitor counting out the number of sheets of ink paper for the number of kids in each row and handed out the sheets to the first student, who then took his sheet and passed the others over his head to the student behind. Ink paper was special in that it was easier to write on than our arithmetic paper.

Next, a blotter was passed out in similar fashion to each student. This envelope-sized piece of cardboard was different in that it was very soft and, as we soon learned, very absorbent. We had already been issued penholders and a metal pen point, which we now fitted together and, oh, boy! We were ready to write.

Miss Gilvere gave her instructions slowly so that each one of us could proceed with the rest of the class. "Gently dip the pen point into the inkwell. Don't mash the pen down to the bottom of the inkwell. Carefully make straight lines or 'ones' on the top line of your paper. Notice that the ink is wet. Use your blotter to absorb the wet ink. When the pen runs out of ink, gently dip it into the inkwell again. Now, let's make circles, and now practice writing your name. Don't forget to blot your work frequently."

Miss Gilvere wandered about the classroom checking on our progress and wondered aloud how some of us boys had gotten ink on our pencils, which, with an amazing lack of foresight, we had left in the pencil slot on top of our desk. She really was a pretty sharp lady and didn't miss much that went on in the classroom.

And so it went with just a few complications for the next half hour. Carl, who always was a bit clumsy, and a couple of other kids had collected too much ink on their pen points and had dropped a blob or two of ink in the middle of their paper. Their blotters proved to be a handy tool, quickly sopping up the excess ink.

At the end of the lesson, Miss Gilvere congratulated all of us on the fine progress we had made in our first experience in writing with ink. She told us we would practice writing with ink several times a week.

The lesson wound up by us wiping our pen point carefully on the blotter to remove all traces of ink, and then we were reminded to close the little door over the hole in the inkwell cover. We were also reminded that our paper for that day was practice only and we didn't need to keep it. That was a relief, especially for Carl.

Big Ink Day had come and gone, and we had survived. Some of us still had questions about the importance of this new technique and wondered if learning to make slingshots wouldn't be a more practical learning experience. The county schools office and Miss Gilvere apparently didn't think so.

Chapter 8

A Lesson From the Okies

One vivid and surprisingly instructive memory that points out the poverty of the Depression years concerned one of the thousands of families migrating from the devastation of the Dust Bowl in the Midwest. These were "Okies" from Oklahoma or Arkansas or Texas who had the hope and need of finding work in the agricultural harvests in California. Most of these families had packed everything they had in or on their car or pickup truck and left their drought-stricken homes to come west to California and its Central Valley and Denair, where I lived.

The kids from these families came to my school, and we were met with regional and cultural and economic differences. It soon became obvious that both groups learned from each other, and some of those lessons were not easily learned.

Garvin was an eighth grader, one of those Okies, probably a couple of years older than the others in his class, and he had four or five siblings, all of whom attended our school in Denair. I was a sixth grader and likely would not have noticed Garvin, except for his amazing duty that he performed regularly.

At noon we all gathered in the lunchroom to enjoy our sack lunches, except for the students who went home for lunch. Garvin would buy a large loaf of bread on his way to school, and he brought a bucket of lard from home. With his younger brothers and sisters seated around him at a table, he would spread one piece of bread at a time with lard, using his pocketknife, and fold that slice of bread to make a sandwich, which he then handed to one of his siblings. He repeated this until all of the kids had their sandwich. Then he did the same for himself. This was their lunch.

I don't recall hearing grumblings or complaints from the kids. I don't recall a look of disgust on Garvin's face, but I noticed the deliberate care he showed while attending to his family. This was a poor Okie family, and we of the "higher strata of society" (as we considered ourselves for a brief time) tended to look down on these interlopers, these Okies, but here was one inspiring guy demonstrating an awesome responsibility to his brothers and sisters as if he were their parent.

I remember talking with some of my classmates about Garvin and what we saw in the lunchroom. We thought the lard thing was a little strange, when we had Nucoa (margarine) or peanut butter and jam on our sandwiches, but we found nothing to laugh about or snicker about.

We couldn't help but be impressed by the way Garvin went about taking care of his siblings. He did it without fanfare or embarrassment. It was something that needed to be done, and he just plain did it. Our respect for Garvin, and for Okies in general, reached new levels and we learned something about acting in a mature manner from just a poor ... from one of the students in our school.

Historical note: The Nucoa that most of our families used came without the butter color. Instead, there was a little packet of coloring that we would sprinkle on the pound of Nucoa and we kids would vie for the privilege of mixing the coloring into the Nucoa. Then there was the pound of Nucoa in a plastic pouch, which included a color bean that we would break and knead in the pouch to distribute the color. Think of the poor kids who came from families that had a cow or two and had to put up with eating real butter and missed out on this privileged task!

Chapter 9

Movie Days

"Paul, did you know we are going to have a movie today?" Annabelle seemed eager to share this bit of information with me as soon as I got to school. Annabelle was a really smart girl who always seemed to be in the know, and she was cute. I was happy to get the news because movie days were big stuff for us fourth graders.

A few minutes later I ran into Art. "Hey, Art, guess what? It's movie day, Mr. Gripinstraw day." He quickly picked up on the excitement of the day: "Hip hip hooray, Gripinstraw day!"

Mr. Gripinstraw was the man from the county education office, the man who brought the movies, and the man with a magical name that captured our attention. We had a good variety of family names in our school. We had Larson and Doerksen and Johnson. We had Sousa, Silva and Vierra. But for some reason, maybe the reasons just listed, the name Gripinstraw was special. It was unusual and it was fun to say and it related to all of the good things that seemed to happen on the days he came to school with his movies.

First of all, we liked Mr. Gripinstraw because he was friendly with us and friendly with the teachers. And we were intrigued by the whole process when he set up the projector, threaded the film, did the rewind and all of that technical stuff. Sometimes he let us carry an extension cord or some other piece of equipment.

An unusual feature of movie day was the fact that our lunch room, the largest room in the school, could not be darkened to show the movies, and the solution to this problem only added to the excitement of the day.

Arrangements had been made with Friends Church, right across the street from the school, to serve as a movie theater. They had drapes over the windows of the sanctuary, which could be closed to darken the room. At the appropriate time, three or four of our classes lined up, and in more or less an orderly file, marched from the school, crossed the road and took our seats in the church pews where we waited for the show to begin.

Sometimes Mr. Gripinstraw would introduce the movie and tell us what special things to look for. Other times, one of the teachers would introduce the program by first reminding us to be on our best behavior because we were guests of the church and were all thankful to Friends Church for allowing us to use their sanctuary for the movies. Most of the kids attended either Friends Church or one of the other two churches in town every Sunday, so we had a pretty good idea of what was decent behavior in church.

And these movies were amazing, not like the ones

some kids went to see on Saturday, like Mickey Mouse or Snow White. We saw for the very first time the way real people lived in the African jungles and the Australian outback. We saw Niagara Falls and the glaciers in Alaska. We saw the homes of Indians who lived in our own country, teepees of the nomadic tribes of the Great Plains and the hogans of the Navajos in the Southwest. These were exciting adventures and watched in often stunned silence at the wonders of the world we lived in.

Later, back in our classrooms after the movies and after a short recess, we talked about what we had seen and heard about other places and other people. While most of us agreed that it would be exciting to see those foreign places firsthand, we were all thankful for the way we lived in our town with our families. We had food to eat. We had warm clothes. We had friends and neighbors. We had our churches. We had our school. We had our town and our state and our country. And we had movies with Mr. Gripinstraw.

We were thankful for all of our blessings and for America.

Chapter 10

Kites

Fun in the Wind

"Oh boy, look at that secret note scoot up the string. This one might make it all the way to the kite. Good one!" Not all of our little pieces of torn newspaper—the secret notes—that we had cupped and formed around the string behaved the way we wanted.

All sorts of problems could creep into our manufacturing process. A knot in the string could catch the note and hold it. The little hole we made in the paper (the secret part was whatever our imagination conjured up) might have an extra tear that got caught on the string, or we hadn't fastened the torn paper together quite right to form the wind-catching cup that carried our hopes and notes to the clouds.

But getting the note all the way to the kite was not the only point of our play. It was just fun to play with the kites in the wind, adjusting the amount of bow of the cross stick, and changing the length and weight of the tail (usually made up of old cotton dress strips) that would affect the stability or maneuverability in the flight of the kite and also determine how high it would go.

Kite day at school was one great day. We knew we would have a lot of fun with our kites. This was an event! It took one whole spring afternoon. The parents came and the neighbors came. We knew the parents of the Japanese kids would be there with the beautiful and creative kites they helped their kids make. The bright colors and unique designs by one of these families were usually rewarded by winning the prize for the most outstanding kite, and there was no argument from any of us.

We learned to understand the different customs of our Japanese neighbors, but we could not understand why some of these same families were later taken from us during the war and sent to internment camps.

There were also prizes for the smallest kite that flew and the biggest kite that flew. A lot of us were more interested in the prize for the kite that flew the highest. Mr. Johnson, my sixth grade teacher, had a way of triangulating a kite to determine its height. Here, pretty was not the goal, but how far up in the clouds you could get your kite to fly, and the competition was fierce.

Each of us was convinced that our technical kite making abilities would achieve the highest flyer. We put just the right amount of curve to the cross stick, and the right amount of tail—too much weight can hold the kite down, but not enough weight could make its flight erratic. So we watched Mr. Johnson very carefully as he sighted up his clipboard to each kite and then marked where the string from one corner of his clipboard hung down. This was serious!

If the highest flying kite winner was a boy, we guys made quite a loud ruckus. If the winner was a girl, we were uncommonly subdued and tried to ignore the ladies' cheers.

This was a big, fun day for all of us, the whole community. There must have been 50 kites or more in the air at one time, a stirring sight. Some kites flew well; some didn't. Most of them were brought back down and saved for another day of kiting. Invariably, several of the kites would break loose and sail off into the distance, and some of those would be retrieved from a nearby orchard or field and repaired for the next flight.

Just one other memory about kites: One kite I made did not fly, nor was it intended to. I don't know what prompted this inspiration, but I made a kite that was at least 3-1/2 feet high and covered not with tissue paper, but with butcher paper. It was heavy.

On a windy day I took that kite and pulled my wagon a couple of blocks up the street into the wind. I got into the wagon and held the kite on my back and was joyously and triumphantly transported down the street, through intersections with or without stop signs. I could only hope that if cars were coming, they had working brakes because I did not. I drew the attention of some of the neighboring kids who soon came with their wagons, eager to enjoy the wind power of my amazing kite.

Traffic was light in my little town. All of us survived to play another day.

Chapter 11

Myrna, the Saint, and Harry, the Scoundrel

I am still puzzled how two of my sixth grade classmates, so decidedly different in many ways, could significantly contribute to two highly charged classroom scenes that are firmly etched in my memory. And those scenes likely adjusted the thought processes of each of us in the classroom that autumn.

It might have been the alignment of the Zodiac, or the dust from the almond harvesting—no, too late in the year for that—or possibly the intervention of the Almighty. I just do not know. But I am telling you that the good, the bad and the ugly blended together and taught two not-soon-to-be-forgotten lessons to 23 impressionable kids.

First of all, Harry Dillon is a boy and Myrna Sanchez is a girl, a difference that is appreciated by every red-blooded American girl and boy. But there is more. Harry was a year or so older than the rest of us. He was bigger, a little wiser, a bit more aware. Harry was not a bully. He did not have to prove himself. He was smart enough; even though he frequently missed assignments, he didn't seem to be bothered by that.

The rebellious spirit that lies mostly dormant in young boys found its subtle, and fortunately nonbelligerent, way into Harry's independent lifestyle. We boys liked Harry, not in spite of, but because of his unconventional ways. We wished we could take on more of his self-assured attitude. Harry was our man!

Myrna Sanchez came to our school with a couple of strikes against her. She enrolled two weeks after school started. She was from Oklahoma—an "Okie." Her family, like thousands of others, fled the "Dust Bowl" (severe drought) of the Midwest to find work in the agriculture industry of the West.

Okies were considered just a little lower than us natives. We were of the upper crust—what a joke. Financially, most of our families would be in the same class as the proverbial church mouse. Remember this is in California's rural San Joaquin Valley in the early 1940s.

But Myrna had some good things going for her. She was a tall girl and really quite attractive, though that was hardly noticed by us boys very much. Her clothes were not the latest fashion, but were always clean and pressed. She was bright, friendly and polite, but the most noticeable trait that set her apart was her regular use of "yes, ma'am" and "yes, sir."

We sophisticated Californians weren't quite sure if that was a good thing or a bad thing. We played with the expressions and snickered some about it until Mr. Johnson, our teacher, sensed the ridiculous banter about this issue and promptly addressed it.

He talked about the differences in the people in our country and right here in our town. We were Swedes and Mexicans and Germans and Portuguese and other mixtures. But we were all neighbors and all citizens of our town, state and country. We should be aware of and accepting of folks who might do things a little differently than we do.

Looking at Myrna, he said, "In California, we don't often say 'yes sir' and 'yes ma'am,'" and then, directing his attention to the rest of the class he added in a slow and measured voice, "but maybe we should." What is this? Mr. Johnson thinks this is a good thing?

With a twinkle in his eye, he puts legs to his suggestion and presented this audacious plan to us: He challenged us to try it out on our own parents that very evening. "When your mom or dad asks you to dry the dishes or clear off the table or take out the garbage, rather than mumbling 'Okay, Mom,' just clearly say 'yes ma'am' or 'yes sir.' You might have to pick them up off the floor, but just do it."

To some of us, it sounded like a bit much, but led by the girls (why do they always have to be the ones?) there seemed to be a growing acceptance of the challenge. We just might give it a go.

The next morning, Mr. Johnson and Myrna were anxious to hear the reports on how the experiment had been received. In short, the parents of kids who had the guts to try it were shocked, surprised and elated. The stock in Mr. Johnson and Myrna rose dramatically. Although these expressions of respect did not become habitual overnight, they began to work their way into our conversations. After a while, it didn't hurt at all to occasionally drop in our newly acquired Southern courtesy.

Soon after this enlightening experience, Mr. Johnson had occasion to be absent from school one day. It will help if you know a couple of things about Mr. Johnson. He was our first exposure to a male teacher. Our parents liked him because he ran a pretty tight ship. We liked him because he ran a pretty tight ship and was fun. He had a great sense of humor, played ball with us at the noon recess, made sure we boys treated the girls with respect, and read exciting stories to us when we came in from lunch.

We had a good thing going with Mr. Johnson, so when our normal school day was changed because of a substitute teacher, the adjustment proved almost more than we could handle.

The usual morning routine was simple and comfortable: We came in when the bell rang, hung up coats and sweaters, put our sack lunch or lunch pail on the shelf in the cloakroom, and enjoyed the mouth-watering aroma of peanut butter sandwiches and perhaps fresh-baked cookies wafting through the classroom. All too often, though, the air was laced with the pungent odor of cow manure on the shoes of a couple of the boys who had to milk their cows every morning.

We then stood by our desks and waited for that week's flag monitor to give the words, "ready, salute." We said the Pledge of Allegiance under the watchful eyes of presidents George and Abe. One of the bright boys in our class said he had it on good authority that

George's picture appears unfinished because he had just come from dinner and had spilled gravy on his coat.

He didn't have another coat, so the photographer just took the picture and erased the gravy. Sounded right to us, but you might want to check a history book. It might not have been gravy; could have been cranberry sauce or hasty pudding.

After the pledge, we sometimes sang the first verse of "My Country 'Tis of Thee," then usually took our seats and started to work on some arithmetic problems Mr. Johnson would have written on the blackboard.

This day there were no problems on the board, so now what? We know that sixth grade boys are born with an innate skepticism about the value of any substitute, and there needs to be something done or said by that sub that qualifies them for their legal position of authority. Wisdom from the fertile mind of a 12-year-old.

Just then Mr. Newsome, our substitute teacher, made his inauspicious debut into our lives with the greeting, "Good morning, ladies and gentlemen." As innocuous and proper and polite as that may sound, and I'm sure our mothers would have beamed at the thought of their little darlin' being recognized as a lady or gentleman, something wasn't right.

It wasn't the "ladies" part that posed the problem. We had some gals, in fact most of them, who were well on their way to earning that noble title. They were nice looking, and were beginning to look like ladies, a major consideration in the unquestioned judgment of sixth grade boys. They were smart—that could be a tad irksome at times—and most of them were friendly and easy to talk to.

No, it was the "gentlemen" tag we were given with no basis in fact. For us, that seemed like a far stretch. Now we boys were a pretty good bunch, for the most part. We had learned basic manners from our parents and Mr. Johnson, but we were still 12-year-old boys. Most of us went to Sunday School regularly, but I don't think the Lord had any of us on the short list for sanctification.

So lurking in the unholy recesses of the minds of several of the more socially-advanced young men, aided and abetted by our unelected but recognized leader, Harry, there rose the burgeoning realization that one, Mr. Newsome had made a most inappropriate assumption—gentlemen! And he sounded a tad on the prissy side when he said it. Prissy did not fit with any bunch of boys from the farm country of California's Central Valley.

As we bent to our classroom tasks, whatever Mr. Newsome had prescribed, there was an undercurrent of whispers and mumbling. Things were not going well. Regardless of the frequent throat clearings by our new man, the noise level increased. This couldn't keep going; something had to give.

And then it came. Mr. Newsome went to Mr. Johnson's desk in the front of the room. He rapped the stapler loudly on the desk and made his momentous announcement: "Cease all conversation, please!"

For the juvenile male contingent in the room, these words took a while to register. Cease all conversation, please? Cease all conversation, please? Had he said, "Pipe down" or "Knock it off" or "That's enough," the message would have been clearly understood—no ambiguity.

To our credit, small account that it may have been, we reluctantly realized the gravity of the situation. We were getting out of hand. Mr. Johnson would be back tomorrow. He would certainly get the word, so pushing our impudence any further would not be a good move.

We had better get with the program, Mr. Newsome's program. We might have been country bumpkins, but we were not stupid bumpkins. However, the effects of the original command still lingered uncomfortably. Cease all conversation, please.

Harry Dillon, the rascal and leader of actions recalcitrant, strolled to Art's desk and in hushed but uppity tones whispered, "Cease all conversation, please." Art, not one to waste an opportunity for mischief, leaned across the aisle and admonished Dick, "Cease all conversation, please." Throughout the day, especially at recesses, the senseless comments went on, with Harry's blessings. We boys relished our newfound roguishness, but we knew it would not sell in Mr. Johnson's regime.

The next day, Mr. Johnson was back—a day of reckoning. Our foolish behavior of the day before had lost much of its glitter. We were sure Mr. Johnson had become aware of our highly questionable shenanigans. He had to know that Harry had been a key figure in our escapade of disrespect, but he also knew Harry had a willing following.

He waited until after lunch to broach the subject. Guilt rode the shoulders of each of us who had participated in the now realized childish behavior. Was Harry going to catch it right there in class? Or the rest of us?

Mr. Johnson spoke of his personal disappointment in the actions of those involved. He spoke of respect for those who do things differently than that to which we were accustomed. He reminded us of our small steps of success we had taken in adjusting to Myrna's "yes ma'am" and "yes sir." He said that wisdom and maturity were required to be able to make sensible adjustments to new situations.

Every sixth grade boy desperately longed to be recognized as wise and mature. The day before we had come up woefully short on both scores. Then, rather than letting the guillotine drop, which our quivering hearts and minds (and scrawny necks) expected and reluctantly admitted we deserved, Mr. Johnson endeared himself to each of us, but especially Harry, with his decision.

"Fellas, listen up," he began. "Regrettable mistakes, even dumb mistakes, can be made by each of us, but hopefully we learn from those mistakes and make every effort to avoid any repetition. I still believe in you and your ability to make things right. I am putting this thing behind us, and we are moving on. I am trusting each of you to do the same. I am writing a letter to Mr. Newsome apologizing for the way he was treated yesterday. I will leave the letter with my signature on my desk during the noon hour tomorrow. If any of you believe that you owe me, and your classmates and Mr. Newsome, an apology, there will be room for your signature as well."

We sat a little dumbfounded. He knew. We had been had. And he was willing to forget it. Wow! His eyes rested on Harry, and we saw him nod to Harry. We looked back at Harry who was sitting, looking sober and relieved, and *he raised his hand.* Harry did not often raise his hand. He just blurted out. But his hand was raised.

At Mr. Johnson's nod, Harry stood, looked directly at Mr. Johnson, and said with a slightly quavering voice, "Thank you, sir." Now we were more dumbfounded. What was happening? What was happening to Harry?

Mr. Johnson paused, a hint of a smile appearing on his face, then walked down the aisle to where Harry was still standing and put out his hand.

There was utter silence in the room.

Harry seemed uncertain what to do; this gesture, shaking hands with an adult, likely was a rare thing in his young life. Then he reached up and took the teacher's hand.

Mr. Johnson, his smile now more obvious, said in a gentle voice, "Thank you, Harry." And then more strongly, "Thank you, sir."

Mr. Johnson went back to his desk and sat down. Harry sat down. Mr. Johnson said, "Let's put our heads down on our desks and relax for a minute or two, then I'll get on with reading our story."

The next day the buzzing of the boys was not the "Cease all" thing, but rather "Are you going to sign the letter?" Most of the guys had made up their minds. Noontime couldn't come soon enough.

As soon as we finished wolfing down our lunches, I went to the classroom with Art and a couple other guys. There on the desk was a hand-written letter to Mr. Newsome. The first signature on the bottom was "David

Johnson, Sixth Grade Teacher." The second signature was none other than "Harry Dillon." My bunch signed eagerly as if trying to throw off a load of sin, or at least a guilty feeling.

At the end of the lunch hour, we all trooped back into the classroom. Mr. Johnson came in right after us, went directly to his desk and picked up the letter. For a long moment he looked at it, surely reading every signature, a smile beginning to spread across his face.

He didn't say a word as he slowly folded the letter, put it in an envelope, licked the flap and sealed it. Then, almost ceremoniously, he took a stamp from the desk drawer, licked it and affixed it to the letter.

Only then did he look at us, his entire countenance radiating with joy and pride. He nodded several times, then pumped a strong "thumbs up" to the entire class and began to clap. It was infectious—all of us joined him. I wasn't the only one who tried to look casual in removing some moisture from my eyes.

The Bible teaches that Jesus was the greatest teacher. I can name eight or ten sixth grade boys who would place Mr. David Johnson just one small step below the Master.

Chapter 12

Daily Vacation Bible School

A major happening in our summer schedule was the annual daily Vacation Bible School held the second week after school was out for the summer. I think the leaders knew we would be a little stir crazy if they started the first week of vacation.

Our VBS program ran for two weeks, Monday through Friday from 9 a.m. to noon. It was held at our Missionary Church, and kids also came from Friends Church, the Nazarene church and from no church. It was a time of learning, fun and excitement.

Most of the leaders came from our church, but some came from the other churches as well. Minor theological differences were put aside for what these dedicated people were doing for us kids. The main idea was to learn about the Bible, some of the exciting stories and the message of God's love for everybody.

Each year a major theme was chosen for the two week session, and one year that theme was nautical—oceans and ships and "Aye, aye sir" and "Ahoy shipmate" and all of that sailor stuff. We learned about port and starboard, left and right. I remember that part because the word "port" has the same number of letters as the word "left." Of course, our lessons featured a number of the boat and ship stories from the Bible, and there are some dandies.

There was Jonah and the whale and the fact that Jonah got tossed overboard because the ship's crew knew that he was responsible for some nasty weather. That terrible weather was because Jonah had run away from God and from what God wanted him to do in the city of Ninevah.

We learned that the message was that we should always do the right thing. But if we didn't, even though there could be some consequences, God still loved us and would help us straighten things out.

Some of us boys were more concerned about how awful Jonah must have smelled after three days in that stinking belly of a whale and then was vomited out. Hopefully, he took a bath before he went on to give a warning to the people of Ninevah.

Another critical story was about Noah and the huge ark that he built. A couple of the teachers took small groups of us out to the bean field next to the church and measured off 450 feet, the length of the ark, longer than a football field, and 75 feet to show how wide it was. That was one humongous ship.

We learned about the flood and the animals going into the ark, and how God protects people who follow his plan and that there are consequences for those who do not.

One other boat story came from the New Testament. It was about the disciples who were crossing the Sea of Galilee when the wind came up and the waves were dumping water into the boat. All this time, Jesus was asleep in the back of the boat. The disciples got all shook up because it didn't look like he cared about their dangerous situation.

But he did care and he calmed the seas and the wind and then reminded the disciples that they needed to trust him and not be afraid. The message to us kids was that we should trust Jesus because he loves us and wants to help us do the right thing.

Vacation Bible School was a fun time for us all. We sang songs, we learned Bible verses and we had "sword drills," contests to see how quickly we could find a Bible verse when we were just given the reference. Through songs, we learned the books of the Bible, even those minor prophets with the funny names.

A special memory from Vacation Bible School is from when I was in the second grade. Four or five of us boys were in a class that met on the church platform behind the old pump organ, the kind that required pumping both pedals to blow the wind through the keys to make music.

Mrs. Amstutz was our teacher. Near the end of the VBS session, after she had been talking to us for nearly two weeks about Jesus' love for us, she calmly asked if we would like to invite Jesus to live in our hearts. That seemed to be a good and reasonable thing to do. So each of us said yes, and we prayed to do that.

I don't recall any sudden revelation of theological truths or any lightning flashes; we just accepted it. The next day while I was out playing, I recall saying to myself, "Hey, I'm a Christian." And that felt pretty good.

Since that day, would you believe I have lived a perfect life? What? No, you wouldn't believe that? You shouldn't. Because that, my friends, could bring some lightning strikes that might be a tad painful.

In truth, my life has had the same ups and downs, challenges and blessings, good choices and bad choices that are true with most of you. But it is comforting to know that Jesus, our creator and the giver of life, is a forgiving and loving God.

The school year just completed was already a fading memory. Vacation Bible School gave us a great time of fun and learning, and now we had a couple of months of summer and as-yet-to-be-discovered adventures before we even began to think about the next school year.

So heads up, here I come with my battered bike, bare feet and a browning skin, ready for a new day.

Chapter 13

Summer Days and Nights

My summer days began with a quick donning of bib overalls—you know, straps over the shoulders and usually with a pair of undershorts. The girls wore dresses. (Imagine! No shorts or pants! But they had dresses for play, as well as dresses for school or church.) We went barefoot most of the time, except on Sundays or when we were "going to town" or having company over.

As we gathered as a family in the kitchen for breakfast, the aroma of Dad's coffee greeted us, along with the gentle smells of Quaker Oatmeal or Cream of Wheat. Shredded Wheat, the "Original Niagara Falls Product," with four layers of three biscuits each was fun to eat, especially because adding intrigue to the cereal were the pieces of grey cardboard separating those layers, each printed with intellectual or artistic challenges.

There were pictures to color or to cut out or facts about transportation or Indians or history. I've learned that some kids did not wait to eat their way through the layers, but dug out the cards as soon as the box was opened to find what challenges they held. I might have done that a time or two.

Sometimes Mom would fix pancakes, which we smothered with syrup made from brown sugar, or a rare treat of Log Cabin Syrup poured from the chimney. That log cabin tin had a life in our playtime far past its syrupy days. We ate other cereals, too, and Tom Mix, in his Western radio show, encouraged us to start our morning with hot Ralston to give us "cowboy energy."

Asking the blessing before each meal—a normal family practice, and each of us kids had our turn—was usually brief. But when Dad, with his Presbyterian bent, did the honors, he seemed oblivious to the dire and immediate nutritional needs of his progeny. It tested our faith and patience, and besides, the oatmeal was getting cold.

Breakfast was when we learned of the day's events—a baseball game, a piano lesson, going to town on errands—and we all knew our chores had to be done first before playtime. Dad was pretty firm on that. But after sweeping the porch, splitting wood, raking leaves or weeding the garden, the rest of the day was mine.

Bike riding with friends, playing cops and robbers, catching ants and dropping them into a doodlebug trap and watching the deadly battle that followed, or stroking a horny toad between its horns to calm him down before he got mad and squirted blood from his eyes were all possibilities.

I spent a lot of happy afternoons swimming in the irrigation canals and a whole morning could be taken up playing marbles, but only "for fun" because Mom didn't want us playing "for keeps" because a kid could lose his whole bag of marbles to a really good player.

Me (middle) with my siblings, Mark and Bette, 1937

Other times I might enjoy looking for targets for my slingshot or BB gun in the vacant lots or alfalfa fields. There I might come across gophers or snakes or feral cats. I might scare up a cottontail or a jackrabbit or possibly even flush a ring-necked pheasant from its well-hidden nest on the ground, or the out-in-the-open clutch of eggs of a killdeer.

We soon learned of the clever ruse of the killdeer to lure us away from its nest by feigning a broken wing as it flopped along the ground, encouraging us to follow.

I also whittled and notched the three sticks necessary to make a "figure 4" trap to use with a box and thus captured a number of birds, along with the occasional cat.

One time my friend Al and I trapped the neighbor's

cat as Mrs. Lindquist witnessed the whole thing from her kitchen window. Neither she nor her cat saw any humor in the event, and my less-than-heartfelt apology, prompted by my mom, followed. Mr. Lindquist later congratulated me on my craftsmanship in making the trap. That felt good.

Then there was always a baseball game, or just hitting flies and grounders. Life was fun, and there were plenty of playmates around. But when at 8:45 p.m. we heard the *whooo, whoooo, whoooo!* of the Santa Fe Streamliner, the California Zephyr, we knew we had just 15 minutes to end our playtime and scurry home.

When the kitchen clocks in each of our homes struck 9 p.m., we had jolly well be inside, not just near our home, not just stepping over the threshold, but all the way inside the house. And woe to the laggard who tried to challenge the system—missing the curfew meant no outside play for at least a day. That was hard enough on us, but even worse for the young lad who had waited a bit too long to steal a kiss from a sweet young thing after his buddies had left and was looking forward to a repeat meeting of the lips the next night.

Our summer evenings also had a greater impact on our lives than learning to be on time. It was a common practice in all parts of our country to sit on the front porch in the cool of the evening and visit with the family or a neighbor or two.

I can still see my parents relaxing in a couple of rocking chairs or a squeaky porch swing, and us kids just sitting on the porch steps. These times may have cut short or even replaced our normal evening playtime, but maybe the neighbor kids were busy doing other things or we had just had enough wild, hectic activity for the day.

I'm reminded of the old gospel song attesting to the Bible story that "Noah Found Grace in the Eyes of the Lord." It was at these times that I felt grace in the eyes of our parents. They would often ask about our day's adventures and offer comments and suggestions.

Sometimes it was fun just to listen to the adults talk about a variety of things—the economy, some politics, various ideas that might be helpful to our neighborhood.

The gospel song says that the result of Noah finding grace in the eyes of the Lord was that "he landed high and dry" after the flood. My flood, definitely not comparable to the biblical episode, was just the normal questions of growing up.

Being around the folks in these informal but productive times seemed to land us kids "high and dry," enjoying the secure feeling of our home and our parents' love and concern for all of us. It was a wonderful way to end our day.

Chapter 14

Moses and Mom

Honored Lawgivers

You will recall that Moses carried 10 God-given rules written on stone tablets when he came down from Mount Sinai. In case you don't recall, that's where we got the Ten Commandments.

But you might remember that recently those Ten Commandments have been considered by some to be dangerous for kids and possibly considered hate speech, but I digress.

There was one more unwritten, though clearly understood rule, which strongly influenced our summer lives. My mom produced number XI (11, for those of you who don't know Roman numerals), "Thou shalt thoroughly wash thy filthy stinking feet in the tub before you dare get into bed." We were taught to honor all 11: Love God, love your neighbor, honor the other *do's* and *don'ts*, honor your parents, and wash your feet before bed.

The rationale for our strict adherence to that last item, Mom's edict, did carry a sense of reasonableness. During our day of wandering and exploring, it was not only possible but also highly probable that our feet might encounter an exciting array of filth and odor-producing gunk.

Me and my sister, Bette, barefoot

First, the very ground we trod—summertime in the hot Central Valley—featured dust here, dust there, dust everywhere. A run through an orchard and a step on an overripe or rotting peach brought wonderfully warm juice up between our toes. And if the farmer had recently irrigated, we enjoyed the peach and mud mixture. A dead bird, a road-kill horny toad, the normal droppings of birds, chickens, ducks, horses could all be part of the mix.

If we had stepped on a puncture vine or stubbed our toe, which was an altogether too-often occurrence, there would be some caked blood added to the bare feet, to say nothing of the expectorant of some "terbacky-chewing" farmer.

Yes, I'd have to admit Mom was right: Our feet were dirty—but filthy and stinky? So after we came inside at the end of the day, we marched straight to the bathroom to perform our necessary and Mom-honoring duty.

Now the day is over. We were in on time. The Santa Fe Streamliner had done its job. Our feet were clean. We had done our job. Tomorrow is another day of as-yet-unknown adventure.

And then there is that sweetest thing ... pleasant dreams.

Chapter 15

Main Street

Small Town America

My little town straddling the Santa Fe railroad tracks in the Central Valley of California was typical of dozens of other small railroad towns in the valley. In the mid-1930s, there were still visible signs of the national economic collapse a few years earlier.

Historical note: In 1907, my little town's name was changed from Elmwood to Denair in honor of its most prominent landowner/speculator at the time, John Denair. It is interesting to note that at the age of 14, he enlisted in the Civil War and took part in many of the greatest battles, including Gettysburg, where he was wounded. John also served as a bodyguard to President Abraham Lincoln during the war.

In Denair, there was the "old bank building," an impressive brick structure that just a few years back was a thriving business center, but during my time there, it stood vacant. The bank's value to us kids was not the building itself, but the wide sidewalk that wrapped around two sides of the building that became our roller skating rink.

With few other sidewalks in town, it became the place where we strapped our roller skates onto the soles of our shoes with a roller skate key and dashed off for some fast-moving fun. I'll ignore the skinned knees and bruised elbows that were a regular part of the learning process or from just showing off our not-yet-mastered special moves.

Main Street was about a block and a half long, and most of the town's businesses were right there. The lumberyard was across the tracks, and I think there was an auto repair shop next to that. Our grammar school was on the other end of town just a couple of blocks past the old bank building.

Walton's Grocery, right in the middle of town, was the hub of most of the community's economic activity. It was the biggest store in town and provided for most of the needs of the families. It was a combination grocery store, hardware store, pharmacy and haberdashery.

We could get seeds for planting our garden, a jar of Vick's Vapor Rub, a package of BBs for my BB gun, a new pair of socks when the old pair was beyond darning, Carter's Little Liver Pills and Hadacol. No, probably not Hadacol, a widely promoted "dietary supplement" containing 12 percent alcohol and what was described in Time magazine as "a murky brown liquid that tastes something like bilge water, and smells worse."

No, definitely not Hadacol, but Walton's grocery was

the most convenient place for our folks to chat and exchange information on what was happening around town. "Molly's new baby weighed 8 pounds, 3 ounces."

"How much are we going to get for alfalfa this year?"

"Did you know that Fred got a new Buick Century?"

"I hear that the new fourth grade teacher is very good. Doesn't put up with any nonsense."

"The Doerksens just got that new milking machine rig. George said he is getting too old to mess with his one-legged stool and holding a bucket between his knees."

"We have a missionary coming to our church Sunday who just got back from spending 10 years in Africa with the Sudan Interior Mission." And so it went.

I was the one in our family who often went to the store for a few specific items. Mr. Walton would frequently greet me with, "Good afternoon, Mr. Jennings. Will it be the usual today?"

I'd say, "Yes, sir," and while I was getting a loaf of Kilpatrick's bread from the shelf and laying it on the counter, Mr. Walton proceeded to the meat counter with his little aluminum paddle, dug out a pound of hamburger, weighed it, wrapped it and placed it on the counter next to my bread.

Meanwhile, I was still beaming over that "Mr. Jennings" and thinking Mr. Walton was one amazing guy. I knew that Kilpatrick's bread, "that good bread in the bright gingham wrapper," was a winner because they talked about it on the Lone Ranger radio program. More about that in a bit.

Sometimes I might have cash for my purchases.

Other times there was an intriguing process that followed. Mr. Walton would get out his little receipt book and write down the bread and the hamburger (the usual), the cost of each and the total.

He would give me the top piece of the receipt and then place the carbon copy in the "J" section of a shoebox that had alphabetical dividers. He tossed out the thin piece of carbon paper that came with the two-piece receipt.

The next time Mom or Dad went to the store, they would make a payment on our grocery bill. Mr. Walton would go to the shoebox, dig out the Jennings' receipts and add them up, either with his little adding machine (type in the total amount of each receipt, pull the handle, type in the next amount, pull the handle and so on) or he would lick his pencil and write down each receipt total on another sheet of paper and add up the total.

It seemed like this was even a tad faster than using his trusty adding machine. Just as accurate? My dad never questioned Mr. Walton, nor do I think he had any reason to. I guess that made Mr. Walton the town banker, as well.

Right next to Walton's was the Creamery, with a nice long counter and several tables. It was a popular spot with my brother, Ben, and sister, Mary, and the high school kids.

One afternoon, Ben and I were downtown and he invited me to join him in the Creamery, where he treated me to a milkshake. Big deal? Well, I should hope to shout! Cost him 15 cents, but he was always working a couple of jobs so he had enough money. That was my very first milkshake, and I knew it would not be my last.

Our town's post office was located on the other side of Walton's Grocery, and two items of note stand out in my memory about it. The first letter I ever received in the mail—and right there was my name typed on the front of the envelope—came from none other than the Lone Ranger.

It must've been because he and Tonto, his faithful Indian companion, recognized my eagerness to serve alongside them as a "defender of law and order in the early Western United States." Or it might have been because I had ordered a decoder pin, a special badge, or maybe a silver bullet.

I don't remember exactly what I ordered in my letter, but I remember that it took a 3-cent stamp, and that took some serious pleading with Mom. It was enough that I got a letter back and there it was, right there and it was addressed to me.

Of greater significance was the tamper-proof security system employed by the U.S. Postal Service for our protection. It consisted of two dials on the door to our letter box (our P.O. Box number was 162), each dial containing one-half of the alphabet letters.

Our combination—I hope it's safe to reveal this—was to turn the top dial to H and the bottom dial to U before the box could be opened. No other combination would work.

Did we have concerns about identity theft or cyber invasion? Not on your life. I told you it was tamper-proof. I was convinced that not the Chinese or the Russkies or the Mafia would have figured it out. I wouldn't bet against the Navajo Code Talkers, though.

Across the street from the post office were the beauty shop and the meat market. I had little occasion to be concerned about the first, but a visit to the butcher shop was always a rewarding experience. There usually were a couple of chickens or turkeys and maybe a quarter of beef hanging by the counter, and Joe, the butcher, might be cutting up a beef or even a deer from one of the local guys' hunting trips, or making hamburger.

After completing whatever business I had, probably getting a couple of chickens, Joe would often ask, "How about a bone for your dog?" My dog and I were grateful. Butcher Joe was our friend.

It is interesting to note that liquor was not served any place in our town. There was no bar. That might've been part of the reason that we had no local police. Every once in a while, a police car from nearby Turlock rolled through town, but the concern of us kids was not, "Who got shot?" but rather "Somebody must've stolen a bicycle or siphoned some gas from one of the farmer's gas tanks."

Down on the corner toward the railroad tracks was our town's service station, Web Moore's Service Station, selling Signal gas. We kids liked to hang around the service station because of all the activity going on.

When a car pulled up to the gas pump, Web would first give a "Good morning, Mrs. Green," or "Hi, Dave," and then ask the customer how many gallons of gas he wanted, at 20 cents a gallon. Web would start the pump and while the customer was getting gassed (you know what I mean), he would check under the hood for any oil or water requirements. He would show the oil dipstick to the customer who would see that the oil was okay, or if it was low, Web would wait for the customer to say, "Better add a quart."

Web would then pump a quart of oil from the big square tank that sat on the floor inside the shop. This required cranking the handle on the pump to pump the oil into the special oil can with a handle and a long flexible spout, or else he would get a quart can of oil from the shop and push in a metal pouring spout.

After pouring in the oil, he would bring the dipstick back to the driver so he could see the new oil level. Web's quick washing of the windshield, collecting the money for the gas and oil and a few encouraging words with the driver would end and the transaction would be complete.

I remember Dad and most of the other customers briefly chatting with Web about local or national news. Web was a well-liked and respected member of our community.

But more importantly, Mr. Moore was our friend. The frequent flat tires on our bikes, often caused by the goat head thorns of the puncture vines, required patching the inner tube. Most of us knew how to change our bike tires and apply the patches, but if we had problems, Mr. Moore was willing to help us—a new valve stem or maybe even a new tube.

Besides, while we all had tire pumps at home, it was a lot more fun using the compressed air hose at the station to pump up our tires. If we needed to tighten the wheel spokes, Mr. Moore kept a spoke key just for that. One more very good and important thing was that Mr. Moore gave us rubber for our slingshots from old bike inner tubes.

To picture Web's Service Station, think back to some old movies or perhaps *The Andy Griffith Show*, where you might have seen gas pumps that had the glass cylinder at the top of the pump in which the red gasoline was held. Webb's station had two of these pumps.

When the pump was running, it was easy to see the level of the gas going down in the glass cylinder. Numbers on the side of the glass indicated how many gallons were being pumped into the customer's car or tractor. After the transaction was completed, the glass cylinder was replenished by physically working a handle on the side of the pump back and forth until gas was pumped up to the top and ready for the next customer.

Now here is where the tale gets really exciting. Mr. Moore, at times, would let some of us kids do the job of refilling the glass cylinder. Under Web's watchful eye, we would take a deep breath, assume a strong stance and grab that pump handle with both hands, and with steady, full strokes, push and pull the handle back and forth and watch the gasoline being pumped up into the glass cylinder. As we neared the end, Web would usually take over to top it off. That was one fun job, and a thrill every time we got to do it.

We kids knew we had helped keep cars on the road and farmers' tractors ready for the next alfalfa mowing. The valley's struggling economy may have succeeded without the efforts of us boys, but we were content to know that we had helped our town move ahead. And we were thankful for Mr. Web Moore for letting us be part of our town's business.

Any of you who have ever in your lifetime worked a gas handle back and forth, please raise your hand. Or just sit back and enjoy the reflection on one of your own major childhood accomplishments.

Chapter 16

Frequent Freights and Hungry Hobos

As important as it was to our summer evening playtime schedule, the proud, brightly painted yellow and orange Santa Fe Streamliner was not the only train to bring not-soon-to-be-forgotten railroad memories to my valley life.

That sleek modern monster roared through our town twice a day, never stopping for us country folks—hurrying north in the morning and back south in the evening, always in a rush to take important people to their important appointments.

Rather, it was the almost constant rumbling through our town of the freight trains—long, noisy and often smelly freight trains, 15 to 20 of them every day, carrying cows and sheep, tractors and cars, lumber and coal, Army jeeps and tanks, and some free riders—that opened up a world of excitement for us kids. Just living near the tracks was fun.

We walked on the rails to see how far we could go

without losing our balance. We watched the rails dip as the wheels of the train passed over the railroad ties.

Every now and then we found a railroad spike that had worked loose from the track. The track repair guys were usually very prompt in replacing the spikes, and we watched as they pounded in the new spikes with their sledgehammers.

We dutifully waved at the engineer up front in the engine. The fireman, also in the engine, didn't wave because he was usually too busy shoveling coal from the coal car into the huge furnace of the steam locomotive. We always waved at one of the men in the caboose, too.

Yep, every train had a caboose where the conductor or the brakeman or the flagman or maybe all three rode. They had important jobs, like adjusting the brakes or uncoupling a car on a siding or waving the flag at the engineer in the front of the train. One of their assignments must've been to wave at the kids in the small towns along the railroad who were eagerly waving at them, because they almost always waved back.

It was well-known that if a person put their ear down on the rail, they could hear the clicking of an upcoming train as it passed over each joint of rails long before the train came into view or before you could hear the sound of her whistle. We imagined or cheerfully lied about hearing the train 20 minutes before it arrived.

Sad note for kids: The railroad rail makers increased the length of each rail from the normal 39 feet to two or three times that, and sometimes welded each length so that there were far fewer clicks to be heard by young railroad junkies. That was no fun.

Happy note for everyone: This process made the trains safer and more comfortable for the passengers. Win some, lose some.

When we could spare a penny, we put it on the track for the train to flatten it out, even though we knew that was a no-no and there was a danger that we might be put in jail for our action because the train might be derailed.

Although there could be serious consequences for our bold and questionable behavior, I don't remember anyone who ended up behind bars or any train disasters. And it was cool to have a flattened penny.

Historical railroad note: The Santa Fe railroad was officially the Atchison, Topeka, and the Santa Fe. "Atchison, Topeka, and the Santa Fe" has a kind of catchy rhythm to it—a song, maybe? It was years later, in 1955, that the Santa Fe merged with the Burlington Northern Railway Company, and that's why you now see these trains marked "BNSF." The Burlington Northern Santa Fe Railway Company and the Union Pacific Railway Company are the two largest railroads in the nation today.

Another very real and captivating connection of our lives to the railroad was the presence of hobos, a phenomenon of the Depression years. There were hobos before then and hobos for many years after, but the '30s and '40s were the peak years.

The major contributing factors to this mass transit curiosity were the loss of jobs in the South and East and drought conditions (the Dust Bowl) in the Midwest. Folks were being forced to leave their homes, often with little or no money, and for the single person, the railroad offered a somewhat reasonable solution of cheap transportation.

These were desperate times for thousands of people seeking to escape their current situation, always in hopes of finding better conditions wherever the trains took them. For many, the goal was seasonal work in the agricultural harvests of the Western states.

Also found on the trains were adventuresome young men and a few bold gals, would-be hobos, seeking the romantic adventure of "riding the rails." For most, the romance was short-lived. It was a poor, harsh life and few found it rewarding enough to stick with it.

The Bulls—hobo term for police—did not treat these free riders kindly. Extreme poverty and nasty weather made strong arguments against continuing the hobo life.

When I was in the first grade, the dangers of hitchhiking on freight trains became a gruesome reality. Stan, one of my classmates, and his brothers were walking to school one morning along the railroad tracks and saw a human head in the middle of the tracks.

After all the excitement, and there was obviously a lot, we learned that the police confirmed that a hobo had fallen from a moving train and had been run over.

But in nearly every railroad community, there was a bright spot, the home where a traveling man—the regular hobo—could find a touch of hospitality and a bite of home cooking. One of the rays of human sunshine in our little town was none other than my mom and our home. We kids were always puzzled about how these hobos knew about our home.

While we were warned to stay away from the hobo

camp down by the tracks, we were also taught to show respect and caution to the down-and-outers. We would hear the knock on the back door and a plea for a small handout.

Mom's response was often a suggestion for the visitor to do a little work—split some wood, hoe the weeds in one row of corn in the garden—while she fixed something. Then came a welcome plate of leftovers. Wait, that was unlikely. We were five growing kids. Leftovers? The chance of having those were slim to none. Still, Mom always found something, some fruit, a sandwich, and maybe, just maybe, some leftovers.

Often I would volunteer to deliver the plate of goodies to the caller, under Mom's watchful eye. Always polite, always thankful, but not always clean, the hobos were a constant fascination for me, and I looked forward to chatting with them.

They told me of their homes in Tulsa or Wichita or Amarillo, places foreign to me. They told me of the states they had traveled through and the stormy weather they had to put up with, and yet here they were in my little town on their way to somewhere and the promise of a better life.

A couple things about Danny, one of our railroad visitors, made him stand out from any of the others. He said he was from Arkansas, and that may have been true because he had the most outlandish drawl I had ever heard.

When I brought out the baloney sandwich and the peach that Mom had prepared for him, he bowed his head as if he were praying. He told me he lost his job back home because he got drunk too often, but now he had given that up and was following a new life.

I told my folks his story, and some of our doubts were reduced when after he finished his handout, he went out to the garden and hoed another row of corn.

While railroads are still a vital part of our nation's economy, there's no use waving at the back of the train.

There is no flagman any more. There is no caboose.

I'm thankful they were there when I was a child.

Chapter 17

Train Communication Problem

An Exciting Solution

Another adventure in our association with the railroad, and I'll bet this is new to a lot of you, involves this communication challenge: How to pass vital information from the engineer of a moving train to the station agent, or—and this is the good part—how to pass information from the station agent to the engineer of a speeding train. Remember, there were no phone connections and no electronic devices, but the word must get through.

First the hardware. Picture a thin stick, possibly a length of bamboo about six feet long, shaped in the form of the numeral nine (9), or if odd numbers freak you out, consider a six (6).

The loop on the stick is about 15 inches in diameter, leaving the handle about 18 inches long. From the top of the loop to the end of the handle, the total length would be about three feet. Where the loop closes on the stick, there is a clip to which notes could be attached.

Now the process. When the train engineer needed to

deliver a note to the station agent, he simply attached the message to the clip on the message stick and dropped it from the speeding train near the front of the station, where the agent could easily retrieve it. Nothing dramatic; it was apparently effective, but a tad boring when considered by a small group of young but keen observers.

Here's the special nerve-tingling part of the total solution: Getting a note from the station agent to the train roaring through town was another matter entirely, and this got our blood pumping.

The station agent, having attached a critical note to the message stick, would stand near, only three feet away from the track, facing the train that would be thundering toward him at nearly 200 miles per hour. (Well, okay, maybe not that fast. I told you our blood was pumping.)

Ignoring the buffeting winds created by the speeding train and the flying cinders and the dangerous suction that could draw him underneath the train's large steel wheels, the station agent would boldly hold the message stick over his head so that the loop extended up and toward the train tracks and the speeding 10,000-ton monster bearing down on him.

The engineer would move to a lower step of the engine, hold out his arm in a bent position and hook the loop of the message stick with his arm.

The station agent then quickly and wisely moved away from the train.

The amazed young observers cheered at having again witnessed the successful and thrilling, though dangerous (dare I say death-defying?) successful communication.

One more critical element of the story must be told because we kids became more than observers. The train folks, having collected extra message sticks along the way, often dropped them off in the vacant lot next to the agency.

We boys, the ever ready and faithful (though unpaid) ground crew, picked up the sticks and took them to the station agent so he could use them on the next train needing a message. Consider the grave situation in which a necessary message from the agent to the train could not be sent because the station agent didn't have a message stick ready to use.

What if that message was to notify the engineer that there was another train coming in an opposite direction on the same track or maybe (and this was more likely) that there was a dead cow laying on the track ahead? The result could be catastrophic. (By the way, we all thought "cowcatcher" was an appropriate name for that heavy metal iron grate on the front of the engine.)

We boys clearly knew that our able assistance in gathering the empty message sticks and delivering them to the station agent had contributed mightily to the safety and smooth operation of the Santa Fe railroad.

Chapter 18

A Young Warrior's Weaponry and a Life Lesson

Before I was allowed to have a BB gun, much less a .22 or a hunting rifle or a shotgun, the vestigial strains for the hunter instinct began to emerge from the dormancy in my as-yet-undiscovered DNA.

The weapon of choice for a fourth grader back in the day was not the spear or the mace or flaming arrows, but the slingshot. The slingshot, the lowly and often maligned slingshot is described in the dictionary as a "small hand-powered projectile weapon." Some self-righteous moralist added this tarnished view: "a tool for juvenile delinquents," clearly an ominous precursor to a life of degradation and crime.

There have been many of my generation who used slingshots and somehow escaped that prediction, like the many thousands who fought in several wars to preserve the principles of freedom, and the countless men and women who pursued scientific fields and developed almost unbelievable advances in medicine and transportation and communication.

Many former sling-shot enthusiasts later became musicians and athletes who have made lasting contributions to our society and to our enjoyment. And how about the national statesmen, including a couple of sling-shotters who became presidents, including Abraham Lincoln?

Though history records the virtues of its cousin, the sling, used effectively by ancient gladiators, the slingshot history is more brief, since it requires a strong elastic material to provide power, and since Mr. Goodyear did not come up with vulcanized rubber until the late 1800s, the slingshot is a newcomer to the tactical approach of hunting and warfare.

On behalf of a stalwart group of enterprising American boys, as well as not a few brave hearted girls, I accept the responsibility and challenge of promoting a wholesome and un-jaundiced view of our tool, weapon, and sidearm—the lowly slingshot—and champion its seldom recognized merits.

Historical note: The guerrilla group, the Irish Republican Army, included slingshots in their arsenal, and prior to the 2003 invasion of Iraq, Saddam Hussein released a propaganda video demonstrating slingshots as a possible insurgency weapon for use against invading forces.

YouTube calls the slingshot a "do-it-yourself" project. Well, duh! Ordering from you-can-find-everything-here-Amazon came late to this party, about 75 years late. Of course I made my own, as did my fellow buddies and fellow Nimrod warriors.

The construction process was a fun challenge. First, a good forked stick was needed, and the best ones were to be found in the willows that grew down by the Santa Fe railroad tracks near the hobo hangouts. After cutting a fork to fit my hand, I peeled off the bark of the wood, which would become dry and hard. To loosen the bark, I held my pocketknife by the blade and tapped the fork with the back of the knife.

What do you mean, "Where did you get your knife?" Every boy carried a pocketknife.

We used them during school recess to play Mumbley Peg and other games. Next in the manufacturing process of the slingshot was cutting a small ring around the tops of the fork to make it easier to tie the rubber strips on.

The strips are cut from a discarded bicycle tire inner tube, and the best source for those was Web's gas station down at the corner. Then another piece of leather—a tongue from a worn out shoe was ideal but harder to come by—attached to the end of the rubber strips to form a pocket to hold the projectile. The fearless warrior, thus armed, was ready for battle. Tin cans, stray cats and wooly mammoths could become likely targets.

Small rocks were the most available, and therefore the usual ammunition used, but the missile of choice for serious shooting was the playground marble, which flew much straighter than rocks and had better aerodynamics than rough rocks. The Bible's David was surely aware of that when he carefully picked up five smooth stones to do battle with the Philistine giant, Goliath. Served him quite well, as I recall.

Now comes a life lesson. One fine summer morning, my route took me down the town's quiet streets toward the vacant lots behind the old deserted bank building, the one with the skating sidewalk. As I neared my target destination, attention was drawn to the noisy twittering and lively activity coming from a large stand of overgrown pyracantha bushes up against the old building.

There were birds—lots of birds—a whole flock of birds, and not just ordinary birds; these were Cedar Waxwings breakfasting or brunching on the red ripe pyracantha berries. This was special. These birds came through our area only a couple times a year, always in flocks, and didn't seem to visit very long. Yet here they were, right in front of me, doing their thing.

Momentarily mesmerized by the stunning scene, I watched the frantic feeding. Snapping back to reality, I saw the opportunity for bagging a rare trophy. This was far better than a cat or a blackbird.

Out of my pocket came my trusty slingshot. Nervously, I fumbled for a marble, gripped it firmly in the leather holder, slowly pulled back, took aim and let fly.

Straight and true the marble flew, and soon I had in my hand a dead bird with a pyracantha berry still in its beak. It felt warm in my hand. The eyes were open, but there wasn't any movement, not a twitch or a flutter.

My initial elation began to fade on realizing I had just killed something, this bird, a Cedar Waxwing. Had it been a common sparrow (notwithstanding God's attitude toward sparrows), it might have been different. But this was a Cedar Waxwing, an uncommonly beautiful creature with soft, velvety feathers and delicate coloring.

This bird was dead. Its life had been taken away—I had taken it away. It would never fly again. It would never eat pyracantha berries again because of my action in proving my hunting prowess. I sure couldn't tell Mom. I don't think I wanted to tell anyone. It was a good shot, but....

Cedar Waxwings were crossed off my target list. I didn't want to go through this again. Other birds? I'd have to think about that.

Seventy-five years later, this episode is still vivid in my mind when I see a Waxwing and recall that emotional scene. I have come to realize that all life is precious and is to be respected and protected. I understand and participate in hunting and fishing, but wanton killing, killing just for sport or convenience, is another matter.

Food for thought.

Chapter 19

Free Haircut Anyone?

Let's see, at 50 cents a haircut, and three boys getting their ears lowered, that's a buck and a half. Hamburger at 25 cents a pound—let's skip the haircuts and we can get enough hamburger to feed our family for a week.

That thinking must've entered the minds of my folks and a lot of other families in the neighborhood. I'm not sure how that played out for other families, but for us, Dad became the barber, and he was the barber for me and my brothers for all of our growing up years.

Dad would announce, "Haircut time," the signal for us to gather in the backyard. Ben, the oldest, would be the first one to climb onto the barber's chair, which was a box on a kitchen chair.

Dad's barber training likely started with Ben, and by the time I came along, his skills had been perfected. He used a comb and scissors and hand-operated clippers—no electricity, just squeeze, squeeze, squeeze the handles repeatedly like garden clippers. As a matter of fact, Dad was a pretty good barber. I don't remember my first store-bought haircut, probably when I was in late high school. And that haircut cost me money. Welcome to the real world.

Me, my older brothers, and Dad

When I was in the Martin's Ferry Indian school in the seventh grade (more stories on that in the next section), Dad had a very special opportunity to donate his barber skills again. Dad sometimes came to the school and offered to give the boys free haircuts. Haircuts were not given a high priority in most Indian families, and as I recall, all of the boys accepted the offer.

This included Alan, a sixth grader, who was there a short time. Dad started his work cutting hair, and by the time he was finished, there was a lot of dark hair on the floor. Then he did the honors on Alan, who was a towhead, and on me, a redhead.

The resulting colorful display of a lot of dark brown hair and a little patch of blond hair and a little patch of red hair was a rare sight, and the Indians found no end of amusement from the scene.

Chapter 20

Swimming and Watermelons

An Unholy Alliance

"Beautiful, long, warm summer days." That's Chamber of Commerce speak for, "Brother, it's hot today; it was hot yesterday, and it's going to be hot tomorrow."

No matter who is being quoted, that latter description correctly fits the summer weather in California's Central Valley. It's the kind of weather that readily lends itself to lots of swimming for kids and tons of watermelons for farmers.

One of my early swimming holes was Harmon's Drop, which was on a lateral (smaller) irrigation canal about a half-mile from our place. A stark memory of swimming at Harmon's Drop was getting there on Zeering Road in the middle of the day—remember the hot days and going barefoot.

The temperature of the asphalt of the road in the shade of an orchard tree or even the shade in the roadside sand was very warm. The temperature of the asphalt in between the shade of the trees was very hot, as in blister-your-feet hot. We kids soon learned to hustle quickly and lightly from shade to shade all the way to the swimming hole.

Another favorite swimming hole, after we had graduated from learning to swim at Harmon's Drop, was Three Bridges, a couple of miles out of town where the lateral canal branched off the dirt-banked main canal. We rode our bikes to Three Bridges.

As I mentioned earlier, swimming weather was also melon weather. And we had lots of melons in the valley when I was a kid. I don't know how long they had been growing there, but a long time, and maybe forever.

I've heard that they had melons in Egypt around the time of the Pharaohs, about 5,000 years ago, back in Moses' time. We had cantaloupes and Crenshaws, we had Persian melons and Casabas. We had honeydews, and best of all, we had watermelons—big, sweet, juicy, wonderfully messy watermelons, with big black seeds that made for outstanding seed spitting contests.

There was a most delightful combination of weather and agriculture-related conditions at Three Bridges. Almost a half-mile upstream on the main canal, a local farmer had a large field of watermelons. Can you see it coming?

The outline of our caper was this: After playing for a while in the canal, we would hustle upstream along the canal road to the prized patch, carefully select two good-sized ripe or perhaps slightly overripe melons, and toss them into the canal. Then we made our way back down the road and took a short swim to cool down.

This was just enough time for the watermelons to

have floated down to us, and we were convinced that the short trip would have cooled the melons to just the right temperature for our anticipated repast. More importantly, it solved a serious transportation problem—those melons were heavy!

After fishing the watermelons out of the canal, we gathered under the old walnut tree that grew beside the canal and there we dropped each watermelon from a height of about two feet onto the hard road surface.

The watermelons conveniently burst open, exposing the still warm heart, which we broke into several pieces and slowly enjoyed one of the most satisfying eating pleasures known to man, or at least to 10-year-old boys.

We learned that Mark Twain agreed with us, as he wrote about the watermelon: "When one has tasted it, he knows what the angels eat."[1]

My editor insists, as would my mother from her grave, that I share another Moses connection to this story. Did we boys not know about number eight of the 10 Commandments—"Thou shalt not steal?"

That's not likely. Did we boys conveniently forget or just plain choose to ignore God's instructions to Moses on Mount Sinai? Very likely. Choices, choices, choices.

One other watermelon memory adds a hint of social redemption, although it doesn't excuse my part in making poor choices. But it confirms the reality that the normal hard work of farming is a part of life that has its own rewards.

My friend, Art, lived on a farm just outside of town. And whenever I visited him, which was often, I was expected to take part in the normal chores that he did on the farm—sort of earn my keep.

Me and my best friend, Art

One year, Art's dad, George, raised watermelons, and it happened that one of my visits coincided with the time to pick the melons and take them to market.

While Mr. George drove the horse-drawn wagon through the field, Art and I would take turns picking the watermelons and tossing them up to the man in the wagon who then gently laid them down on a bed of straw.

At the start of the project, each watermelon felt fairly light in weight, but that changed drastically by the time we had that wagon loaded. Those rascals got heavier and heavier. And watermelons picked from the vine are dirty and somewhat sticky. The hands and arms and shirts of the picker/tosser, as well as the catcher in the wagon, were soon dark and grungy. This was one time when it was a pure delight to clean up when the job was done.

Art and I then rode with his dad the four miles to town to sell the watermelons. What a special ride—the smell of the horses and the leather harness, the sound of their hooves clopping on the road, the sight of their heads bobbing up and down, and their tails switching at annoying flies. Oh, it was a good ride, even with the sight and smell expelled by the very natural regularity of the team.

Other wagonloads of watermelons and some cantaloupes were gathering at the market. I remember sitting proudly perched on the wagon seat with Art and his dad and greeting other farmers. I felt like I was one of them, and I'm telling you that it felt good.

These melons that Art and I picked were going to be sold by the melon buyers to stores throughout the valley. My folks might even buy one that I picked. I wondered if it would taste as good as the melons at Three Bridges.

Chapter 21

Palatable Pleasantries and Peculiarities

Or What's for Dinner?

"Oh, boy, breakfast here I come!" The gentle but distinctive and mouth-watering smells of "eiredach" wafted through the house, even reaching upstairs where my brother, Mark, and I slept. There was no need to call us twice, not when our favorite, although too infrequent, morning specialty was being whipped up.

That was an appropriate term for making eiredach batter—mostly whipped up eggs, a little milk, a small amount of flour, cinnamon, sugar and other select mystery ingredients. The thin batter (think crepes) when fried on both sides and turned onto our plates to be flavored with butter and syrup or brown sugar became a feast for the gods. Or in our case, the gods took on the unholy likeness of five hungry but very thankful kids.

The tradition and the recipe came with my mom's family from Switzerland. We were most grateful that not all tradition was lost in their relocation.

You're undoubtedly well aware of several other

notable contributions from the land of the Alps. You can sport a finely-crafted and multi-jeweled timepiece on your wrist. You can look fashionably adorned in stylish lederhosen. You can taste the distinctive flavor of an ample slab of holey cheese on your sandwich.

All worthy examples of Swissness, yet for our family they were apparently casualties of the trans-Atlantic pilgrimage. Now pardon me while I close my eyes and conjure up the delight of a plate of Mom-made, just-out-of-the-skillet eiredach. Mmmmmm, good!

Our usual nutritive start to the day might have been hot cereal—oatmeal or cream of wheat or cold cereal, like shredded wheat or cornflakes, or pancakes. We had not yet been exposed to the temptations of Post's Sugar Crisps or Kellogg's Pop Tarts, and it seemed unlikely they would have crept ahead of this delicious Swiss import and its first-place spot in our minds of a fine memorable breakfast.

Even in my early years, it was my grand fortune to taste, and on most occasions totally enjoy, a variety of unusual favorite cultural dishes concocted with love and a good memory by my friends and neighbors.

The Martinez family lived right across the street from us with kids of our own ages. The frijoles and Mexican tacos were standard fare for our get-togethers. The Martinez family always looked forward to their special holiday treat, bunelos, a deep-fried tortilla type pastry that they dipped in syrup. Mmmm. Me gusta bien! Muchas gracias.

A Sunday evening ritual with the Doerksens, my buddy Art's German farmer family, was coffee and zwiebach. Think of hard biscuits or rolls, not the sliced dry toast. This was a two-layer biscuit that would be baked a second time (zwiebach: twice baked), which produced a very hard (break your teeth hard) goodie. The coffee, served in a bowl with sugar and fresh cream from their own cows, was clearly necessary for dipping the zwiebach so that it surrendered to a munchable texture.

This tradition, enjoyed slowly and with jovial conversation, was always a special treat for me. We kids could legally and approvingly have coffee along with the older folks. Typically this was a no-no for kids because it was well-known that coffee would stunt your growth and give rise to other future-endangering maladies. But then, Art was a pretty good-sized boy.

I guess there are always a few exceptions to good science. The coffee that dribbled from the dipped biscuit and onto our chins was an expected and accepted part of the experience. Probably would have made Emily Post frown.

Then, after the meal, Art's dad, George, would relax with another cup of coffee "saucer and blowed." He actually tipped his cup so coffee spilled into his saucer. Then, with steady hands, he lifted the saucer to his lips, gently blew across the saucer, and noisily sipped or slurped the coffee with his eyes closed and then a soft "Ahhh."

The first time I witnessed this delicate procedure, my intrigue was obvious as I had an inquisitive stare and a gaping mouth. George noticed and quietly said, "Poulus, (he had told me this would be my name in the old country), this is the only way to drink and enjoy hot coffee." And he took another sip/slurp. Danke.

None of the rest of us ever considered joining this "old school" tradition, which was seemingly reserved for the patriarch. But many years later, in a moment of reverie, I dug out a saucer, and with hands unpracticed, poured my hot coffee into the saucer, blew gently across the steaming drink and sipped (slurped).

I won't say it was an "ah ha!" moment in my life, but I'll tell you what, I enjoyed several moments of good coffee and a passel of fun memories. I imagined old Mr. George looking down on my miniature adventure and smiling, "Poulus, now you're getting it." I might even try again, when no one is around.

The Scandinavians that I knew in the valley could not survive the holiday season without their cherished "lutefisk." This fish product required a smelly two-day brine (lye) soak and another day to leach out the brine. Then it was slow cooked and served in what was claimed to be a delectable dish.

That opinion was often challenged by non-Scandinavians and by a few honest Swedes. One wag was prompted to offer this ditty to the tune of O Tannenbaum: "O lutefisk, O lutefisk, how pungent your aroma. O lutefisk, O lutefisk, you put me in a coma." It is said that lutefisk, as a holiday treat, is more popular in America than back home in Sweden. Does the term "slow learner" apply here? Taksa meeka!

Some of my Native American friends still hold onto the ancient practice of grinding acorns into flour for baking and cooking. The preparation process—drying, grinding and leaching the acorns—is tedious and time-consuming. The distinctive flavor and texture is something I would need to have more time to enjoy.

One of my own unusual gustatorial delights was freshly-caught and campfire-baked eels, which I enjoyed with an Indian family on the banks of Mad River. I'll give details of this amazing experience in another story.

I still relish the fond memories of unique and enjoyable times with friends and neighbors, savoring the delicious delights of their different cultures.

Chapter 22

Family Literary Lessons

The Fine, and Not So Fine, Arts

Highbrow literary learning it was not. Unless you can fit "Big Black Beetle" and "All Cows Eat Grass" into that category. The classics of literature and poetry, while not staples of our learning, also were not totally ignored. Whimsical and serious writings formed a delightful combination in my home and early schooling.

Mom and Dad naturally had a strong influence on shaping the habits and beliefs of us kids. Dad, because of the need in his early years to work on their Missouri farm, likely completed no more than seventh grade. But as a young man, when he finally broke free from those work obligations, he was drawn to reading and became a student of our country's history and the Bible, especially Bible prophecy.

I can picture him now, sitting in a chair with his stocking feet resting on a block of wood on the open oven door (he always had cold feet), reading to Mom while she was fixing supper. His selection might be some book by a prophetic writer or from one of the prophetic biblical books of Ezekiel or Daniel or Isaiah or Revelation.

He reminded us early and often of the familiar words from the Declaration of Independence: "We hold these truths to be self-evident, that all men are created equal, that they are endowed by their Creator with certain unalienable rights, that among these are life, liberty and the pursuit of happiness."

He related this to the work he was doing with the Indians, and said it held true for all people everywhere. He also reminded us of three tenants of his beliefs:

1) America is a Christian nation.
2) In a stack of books including the Bible, the Bible should always be on top.
3) Our flag should never touch the ground.

He was old school, and he was right on.

In spite of, and maybe because of his generally stern demeanor, Dad thought that this quote from Henry Ward Beecher was worth knowing:

"A man without humor is like a wagon without springs, jolted disagreeably by every pebble in the road."

My mom was given to whimsy and fun times and fun poetry. "Big Black Beetle" carried the message that every person has rights, regardless of size or any other description.

"Grasshopper Green" was one of her favorites, and we kids latched onto it as well:

> Grasshopper-Green is a comical chap;
> He lives on the best of fare;
> Bright little trousers, jacket, and cap—
> These are his summer wear.
> Out in the meadow he loves to go,
> Playing away in the sun;
> It's hopperty, skipperty, high and low:
> Summer's the time for fun!

Most of us took lessons on the piano or some other instrument, and learned about sharps and flats and key signatures and the lines and spaces of the musical staffs: E, G, B, D, F—"Every Good Boy Does Fine," the lines of the treble clef. More in keeping with the interest of us boys were the spaces of the bass clef: A, C, E, G—"All Cows Eat Grass."

We had a piano in our home, and both Ben and Mary played well. Dad, at times, would ask Mary to play a hymn so he and whatever kids were around could sing along. In his rich bass voice, he liked to sing the bass part if there were enough of us to carry the melody. These were fun times.

My piano experience, less than laudatory, was under the watchful eye of Mrs. Hale, a neighbor and a friend of Mom's. I went through the scales and simple tunes and chords, but she set an early goal for me to learn the hymn, "Christ Arose." She assured me that since it was in the key of C, with no sharps or flats, I would soon be able to play it well enough for us to sing it together with my accompaniment.

Well, right away I knew that there were several things that would keep that from ever happening. Mrs. Hale was a good singer with a beautiful alto voice, and since when would a clumsy-fingered 10-year-old accompany an experienced singer?

I knew the hymn because we sang it in church at Easter time. The music for the verses was slow and reverently sung. "Low in the grave he lay, Jesus my Savior, waiting the coming day, Jesus my Lord."[1]

I thought I could handle that pretty well, even though at one place in the bass clef my left hand had to reach beyond an octave, and that was a stretch for me (pardon the pun).

But it was the chorus that came alive in force and tempo and lyrics (forte):

> Up from the grave he arose, with a
> mighty triumph o'er his foes;
> He arose a victor from the dark domain,
> And he lives forever with his saints to
> reign.
> He arose! He arose! Hallelujah Christ
> arose![2]

An angel touched my hands, and overnight I could play like Van Clyburn. Only in my dreams. It seemed like it took weeks of practice and Mrs. Hale's encouragement, but we did sing that song together, she with her gentle alto while I carried the melody and tickled the ivories.

Tickled is probably a good expression of my playing because a number of unscheduled keys were struck and a few scheduled keys were missed. Mrs. Hale was gracious in understanding while we sang the entire song. It was a rare and mighty satisfying experience.

In other literary lessons, Mom tossed in this scientific gem: "Man-Very-Early-Made-Jars-Serve-Useful-Needs-Pluto" referring to the planets in their order from the sun: Mercury, Venus, Earth, Mars, Jupiter, Saturn, Uranus, Neptune, Pluto. This was before some of those astronomer folks demoted Pluto.

Mom also was the one who taught us beginning prayers before bedtime and before meals, and also encouraged us to add our own thoughts and requests to the memorized prayers, so aunts and uncles and presidents and our pets were brought before the Throne of Grace.

Through her efforts and Sunday School and Vacation Bible School, we learned Bible verses and several of the Psalms. The first line of the first Psalm is a happy biblical admonition: "Make a joyful noise unto the Lord." Only a loving and forgiving God would consider some of the sounds of our kids' gatherings to be joyful. Bible memorization became a lifelong habit for many of us.

"You can talk with God even when you're riding your bicycle." That simple statement from my mom was a profound truth that rode with me, on and off my bike, for all of my years. At the time it was filtered through my 10-year-old understanding of praying with head bowed and eyes closed, which really didn't fit except in church when the pastor was praying or at the dinner table when Dad or Mom was praying—certainly not when riding my bike along the canal bank.

I was ready to discount God's interest in my Saturday excursions, but I remember this annoying little song that we learned in Sunday School: "He sees all you do; he hears all you say. My Lord is writing all the time, time, time."

Learning poetry in school at first seemed more of a chore than a pleasure. My fourth grade teacher started off with Ralph Waldo Emerson's "Fable" (a poem we knew as, "The Mountain and the Squirrel"):

> The mountain and the squirrel
> Had a quarrel;
> And the former called the latter "Little
>   Prig."

Well right off the bat, the "former" and "latter" stuff and "little prig" didn't easily fit our normal vocabularies. Do you get a hint of my literary genius? We still enjoyed the lesson of the last few lines, where the little squirrel laid it on the big mountain with these concluding remarks:

> "Talents differ; all is well and wisely put;
> If I cannot carry forests on my back,
> Neither can you crack a nut."

Things got better with Henry Wadsworth Longfellow's "The Village Blacksmith." This was a good story, and we got the feel of how poetry can enhance a story and have a unique value all of its own.

> Under a spreading chestnut-tree
> The village smithy stands;
> The smith, a mighty man is he,
> With large and sinewy hands,
> And the muscles of his brawny arms
> Are strong as iron bands.

We fourth grade boys could only fantasize about that description and then jabbed each other with "the muscles on his scrawny arms are as strong as rubber bands!" Longfellow would have frowned.

In the sixth grade, I got acquainted with another of Longfellow's works, his epic poem, "Evangeline: A Tale of Acadie." Mr. Johnson, our teacher, read the entire poem to us, and it's a long one, and talked about it.

Then in a most dramatic fashion he quoted the beginning lines of the prelude to the poem. Those lines remain with me to this day:

> This is the forest primeval. The
> murmuring pines and the hemlocks,
> Bearded with moss, and in garments
> green, indistinct in the twilight,
> Stand like Druids of eld, with voices sad
> and prophetic,
> Stand like harpers hoar, with beards that
> rest on their bosoms.

Loud from its rocky caverns, the deep-
 voiced neighboring ocean
Speaks, and in accents disconsolate
 answers the wail of the forest.

Poetry, prose and music found a strong and enjoyable place in my early learning, thanks to Mom, Mr. Johnson, Mrs. Hale and Mr. Longfellow, and a whole raft of other creative contributors.

Chapter 23

Before TV and Social Media, There Was Radio

Radio was a key component of our daily lives. There really was life before television.

The radio broadcast, *Evening News* by Gabriel Heater, kept us (mainly Dad) aware of the national and world news. I do remember the evening news reports of our bombers, B-17 Flying Fortresses and B-24 Liberators, dropping their destruction on Germany.

A devastating part of those reports was the number of our bombers shot down by the anti-aircraft fire of the Germans. Death and the ravages of war became real.

Jack Armstrong, the All-American Boy was a regular after-school radio program. On Saturday nights, when my brother Mark and I had gone to bed, we tuned the radio in our room to the *Grand Ol' Opry* and heard the wildness of the Hoosier Hotshots or the more tempered strains of Roy Acuff and the Smokey Mountain Boys singing "The Great Speckled Bird." It branded us as country music lovers for life.

There was *Amos and Andy*, a comedy about black

characters featuring the virtues of friendship, persistence, hard work and common sense; it would probably be considered politically incorrect these days. *Lum and Abner* ran the Jot 'em Down Store and Library. We enjoyed the ridiculous spoofs and good, clean humor.

This was the Golden Age of radio, and my family enjoyed a variety of programs. *Dick Tracy* and *The Shadow* were stirring detective/mystery shows, but for rollicking, outrageous comedy, we liked *Fibber McGee and Molly, Jack Benny, Burns and Allen* and others. Outstanding classical music came into our homes with *The Voice of Firestone* and *The Bell Telephone Hour.*

My favorite was *The Lone Ranger* on Friday evenings. My dad and brother shared my taste in the program. This was the real thing, a heart-stirring avenue to the past. In the fifth grade I was just getting into the early western and frontier life of our country.

Listen to the dynamic narration that opened each episode of *The Lone Ranger*:

> *A fiery horse with the speed of light, a cloud of dust and a hearty Hi-Yo Silver! With his faithful Indian companion, Tonto, the daring and resourceful masked rider of the plains led the fight for law and order in the early Western United States. Nowhere in the pages of history can one find a greater champion of justice. Return with us now to those thrilling days of yesteryear. From out of the past come the thundering hoofbeats of the great horse, Silver. The Lone Ranger rides again!*

Folks, it just doesn't get any better than that! I was ready to strap on a six-shooter gun and go after the bad guys.

The secret decoder pins from some of the kids programs—Tom Mix, Little Orphan Annie, Captain Midnight and the Lone Ranger—offered a level of intrigue to their programs. With a decoder pin, which was sponsored by Ovaltine (hot chocolate) or Kix cereal, you could decipher a secret message given in one episode that revealed a clue to the following episode. As long as one of the kids in the neighborhood had a decoder pin, we were "in the know" about what was coming up next.

All of these radio programs championed good behavior and doing the right thing, even when going through tough times, as we did through the Depression and World War II. These lines from an old poem, "Christmas Bells," that were later used in a familiar Christmas carol, carry the essence of the message of the times: "The wrong shall fail, the right prevail, with peace on Earth, good will toward men."[1]

On Sunday afternoons, we often tuned into Charles E. Fuller and *The Old Fashioned Revival Hour.* This was mainly the request of Mom and Dad, but the way Rudy Atwood, the amazing piano accompanist, tickled those ivories for the outstanding male quartet, it demanded the attention of us kids. Maybe I'd better practice some more for my next piano lesson.

Section Three

Back to Indian Country

Bears, Outhouses, Skunks, & Baked Eels

Humboldt County, Martin's Ferry

1942-43: 7th grade, Martin's Ferry School

1943-44: 8th grade, Blue Lake Grammar School

Chapter 24

A Surprise Move

Right out of the blue. No warning. Well, I'm sure Mom knew and probably Ben and Mary had been told. But it was news to me when Dad made the sudden announcement that we were moving back to Humboldt County. And we only had about three weeks to get ready before we moved.

I had just completed the sixth grade. I was looking forward to a summer of fun with my buddies: swimming, biking and maybe making a little money picking up peaches. I was beginning to enjoy the comforts and security of "small town America." Well, okay, it was in the Central Valley of California during the Depression years, and living was a little lean for most of us. But we were leaving it for "no town America."

Martin's Ferry, our destination on the Yurok Indian Reservation, wasn't even a town; it was just a place. There was no store there. There was no service station. There was no church. They didn't even have electricity, for crying out loud.

Oh, I know, we had lived in Humboldt County before that, but we had left there when I was 5, so I had a few memories, but no real emotional ties to the Indian country. Mom said Bette and I would be in an Indian school and she would be the teacher. Mark would be going to the high school in Hoopa. Still, I wondered about those Indians.

Over the last couple of years I had been reading about the early West, mountain men, primitive living, Indian problems, hunting, trapping and all of that. That was in books, and the stories had given me excitement and the desire for adventure.

I wondered how much of that adventure I would find in this new move to Martin's Ferry. And would it be safe? Could these Indian kids really bury a hatchet in a tree from 25 paces? How friendly would they be to a white kid like me? It was hard to put all this together.

Some of the kids in my sixth grade class had started first grade with me. We were practically family. I knew a lot of the men in town. I'd miss Mr. Walton, owner of Walton's general store, and Joe the butcher who regularly offered a bone for my dog. Mr. Webb Moore, the service station owner, was always friendly with us kids.

One thing I wouldn't miss was having Pastor Grable stop in the middle of a sermon, as he did one fine Sunday morning, to tell his son Joseph and me, "Joseph, you and Paul, you boys straighten up right now."

A couple of dear old saints at the end of the pew stopped their fanning and frowned/glared at us as if to say, "Such shameful, disrespectful actions will surely lead to...." And we were hardly ... oh, never mind. All of this would soon be gone.

Now the move to a new area, new home, new school —how was this going to turn out? I think you will enjoy the stories ahead.

Chapter 25

Martin's Ferry

Our New Home

The sun was setting early behind the big mountain on the other side of the river. There was the Martin's Ferry Bridge spanning the Klamath River and connecting to the Bald Hills Road, which went up over the mountain to the town of Orick on Highway 101, some 40 miles away. That road had been important to our family seven or eight years earlier when we lived in Pecwan.

There was an afternoon haze in the canyon as I looked up the river toward Weitchpec and Hoopa, the way we had come, and downriver toward Pecwan.

I stood there trying to grasp the reality of where I was and what I was doing here. And right there in front of me was the Martin's Ferry Hotel, a very old two-story structure that was to be my new home. In the distant past, it had been painted white, but it showed little sign of having been refreshed or even any signs of recent occupation.

Just a couple of days before, my family had finished

packing away our essentials—clothing, kitchen utensils and some food, garden tools, beds, tables and chairs—everything we could get into the old truck that Dad had found for the move.

I made sure in packing my things to include my baseball glove. But now, looking around at my new mountain home, I saw no flat land that could accommodate even an infield. Maybe flies and grounders if we didn't hit the ball too hard.

While coming through Hoopa, we had stopped at the Brizzard store to stretch, and so dad could see his old Indian friend Ernie Marshall, the proprietor of the store.

Ernie was one of the most beloved and respected men in the area. His ready wit and humor came out when Dad asked about the condition of the road from Weitchpec down to Martin's Ferry. "Roy," he advised, "it's a regular 'boolyvard' down there." And then to clarify, added, "They've really fixed it up pretty good." It was true—the one lane dirt road had no slides or washouts. It was fixed up pretty good.

What had impressed me about that section of the road, in addition to the sharp turns and steep hillside, was that I saw no homes along the way. There were a few faint roads disappearing into the woods, but no homes were seen. Were there really people living here?

Standing in my new front yard, I still saw no neighbors, but there were about two dozen chickens strolling about.

In the 20 minutes since our arrival, I had more questions than answers about our home. Annie Jacobs, an elderly Indian woman who was our landlady, had come out of her house that was adjacent to and only slightly smaller than the hotel, to welcome us.

While she was showing my folks their new quarters, Ben came up with the idea that we three boys could set up our beds outside under the big oak tree. When Annie heard of our plan, she reminded us that the chickens roosted in that tree. Perhaps sleeping under the stars would be a tad less messy.

For the next several weeks or so we did our best to get acquainted with the area and get settled in our new home, but that had some complications because we knew more family changes were coming.

Ben would soon be off to college in southern California. Dad had to assume his church responsibilities in Blue Lake and would be living there. Mary would join him so she could find work in Blue Lake or Arcata and could assist Dad with his church work. That meant we three younger kids and Mom would set up housekeeping in the hotel.

Mark and I soon learned there was a good swimming hole in the river below our place, even though it presented some challenges that we didn't have in the main canal at Three Bridges.

We were both good swimmers, but the river was about 100 feet wide with a deep, strong current. We swam across a couple of times, but soon decided not to push our luck, and instead enjoyed staying in the eddies near the shore on our side of the river.

We also learned that Pine Creek, across the river and about a mile upriver, was not only a beautiful mountain stream, but also was populated with some healthy and hungry rainbow trout.

A month later we were still making progress in adjusting to our new surroundings, such as the nighttime creaks and moanings of the old hotel. No, we didn't think it was haunted. The sounds were softened by the frequent gentle hootings of the owls.

Fixing our meals on the wood stove was more fun reading about it than actually doing it. But we had new schools to face and new kids to meet. We were in Martin's Ferry and we were cautiously excited about our new life there.

Chapter 26

Martin's Ferry Hotel

History and My Life There

There is a significant link between the Gold Rush in northern California in the mid-1880s and my neck of the woods in Humboldt County in my early history.

This is not a history book (do I hear cheers?) but check this out: You will recall that gold was discovered at Sutter's Mill in 1848, and when the word got out to the world, every creek and river in northern California was assumed to be connected to the Mother Lode.

The grandest and most bodacious gold rush in history exploded in 1849. Now you remember the 49ers (no, not the football team)—the men who swarmed the state in that year looking for easy golden riches. (California became a state in 1850.)

My corner of northern California along the Klamath River was not immune to the infectious gold fever that gripped our nation. The frenzied rush to the goldfields on the upper Klamath River brought about some creative adjustments to a very difficult route to the area sought by the fortune seekers.

From Orick on the coast, the miners with pack trains loaded with mining gear crossed over the Bald Hills Road to the Klamath River, where a man named John Martin saw a need and filled it. In the mid-1800s he built and operated a ferry to get the mules and donkeys and men and supplies across the river.

John Martin's ferry on the Klamath River

The ferry has been described as a "well-built cable-controlled flat boat, powered by the current of the stream and capable of carrying a train of seven or eight pack mules and the drivers."[1] The ferry operated until 1917 when a bridge was built, making the ferry obsolete. Historic records also show that an Army fort was built in Martin's Ferry in 1853, and a post office operated there from 1863-1891.

About those pack trains[2]: "The early settlers of

northern Humboldt, Klamath and Siskiyou counties were supplied with provisions, furniture and gold mining equipment brought in by pack trains. These trains usually consisted of from 30 to 40 mules, each mule carrying an average of 300 pounds. A bell mule led the pack train. (The mule had a bell on it to signal help if it got off the trail.) There's also a mule for each packer. The crew consisted of a boss packer, a packer for each 10 mules, and a bellboy who served as cook and led the kitchen mule. During the trip the men subsisted on pancakes, bread, bacon and beans."

The Martin's Ferry Hotel was built in the late 1850s —few records confirm an exact date—on a large flat area on the hillside several hundred feet above the ferry crossing. A corral, a blacksmith shop and several outbuildings were added to accommodate the pack animals and the pack train personnel and other travelers.

The hotel for miners was a two-story building with four rooms upstairs and three rooms downstairs, plus a larger lobby/office/parlor room on the ground floor. A potbellied stove in this room supplied the heat for the entire building. Air conditioning? That's easy: Open the doors or windows to enjoy the cool river breeze. It had a cedar shake roof, and the double outside walls were about 18 inches thick to provide a measure of insulation.

The bridge that later replaced the ferry was built, but the name, Martin's Ferry, stuck.

The century-old hotel became my home in 1942, and my seventh grade year was spent in this historical setting. More recently, I discovered that in 1928, there was some trouble in the quiet community.

According to the Humboldt Historian, a man named Marion Rube had robbed a bank several miles away and made his escape. Twelve days later, "on a dark and raining Sunday night about 8 p.m. ... at Martin's Ferry, retired rancher Arthur Tomlinson stepped out of the front door of his house. As he started for the nearby hotel, gunfire erupted from a clump of trees across the road. As Tomlinson fell, the assailant fired through the windows of the two-story hotel, shattering windows and shooting through walls."[3]

Hey, that happened only 14 years before I was living in that hotel and was looking through those same windows, now fortunately replaced, that had been shot out by Marion Rube!

Officers later "confirmed that Rube was responsible for the robbery of the Weitchpec store and that he had killed Tomlinson by mistake. Rube told his friends that he had intended to kill Tully (a deputy sheriff who had tried earlier to capture Rube), and that 'I'm sorry I killed Tomlinson, but I will get Tully yet.'"[4]

Two months later, Rube, who was called one of the "state's most notorious criminals" died after being shot by citizens following another hold-up and attempted escape.

In the years between the murder of Tomlinson and our occupation, the hotel had less activity, and in the two to three years before our arrival, it probably only housed some wasps and a few squirrels.

In Denair, we had our icebox. In Martin's Ferry, we didn't have one, for the simple reason that there was no ice available. Instead, my dad constructed an evaporative cooling unit that had a charm of its own. A year-round spring, a short walk from our back door, provided the refrigerant—water piped in from the spring—that trickled over a burlap-covered screen box.

Milk (unless the cow was dry), butter or Nucoa, eggs (when we could find where the chickens had laid them), veggies and other goodies, and wild blackberries and huckleberries in season were kept fresh and edible in the special screened box.

We occupied two back rooms on the first floor of the hotel—the only occupants in the place. We had a small woodstove for heat and cooking and a unique kitchen set-up—no sinks or running water, but a long wooden counter on which our pans and pitchers of water sat.

I remember Postum (instant coffee) and tea and Carnation canned milk for cream and diluted canned milk for our cereal. Spam and beans were standard fare, and on the weekends when Mom went to Blue Lake to be with the rest of the family, she would bring back soups and stews for our meals.

Occasionally I would provide trout from the local creeks, and the time that Billy (you'll hear about him in a minute) and I shot a deer, venison was on our plates for a while.

The outhouse was also out the back door, but away from the spring. Kerosene lanterns and candles provided our light. This may sound like a grim lifestyle, and it was, but I don't recall that Mom or I ever grumbled about it.

The bridge across the Klamath was taken out in the flood of 1955 and the new "modern" cement bridge was built. To accommodate the realignment of the road and the approach to the bridge, the old Martin's Ferry Hotel and all of its outbuildings were torn down and a hundred years of history wiped out.

Another chapter in my life closed, but rich memories remain.

Chapter 27

New School, New Friends

One of the earliest and most urgent curiosities that my sister Bette and I had concerned that "one room school" that we would be attending, so only a few days after our arrival, Mom went with us to check it out.

Martin's Ferry School

We walked the dusty half-mile down the road to a driveway that led 30 steep yards up to the school. I'm not sure what I was expecting, but this was a sight to behold. At one end of the big dirt schoolyard, which was snuggled up against the hillside, we saw the school, a small, rather neat looking building with a friendly porch across half of the front of it.

At the other end of the schoolyard, confirming the reality of our new primitive living conditions, was the outhouse—the school's bathroom.

In between these two buildings, there was just a dirt play yard, which was somewhat rocky. There was no playground equipment, no monkey bars, no basketball hoops, and clearly no baseball diamond. This was not like my school in Denair. I remember thinking, "Wow, this is just like the olden days." And this was now my school. Was I really ready for this?

We walked over to the school building and I took a seat on the porch bench that was so inviting. It was a nice place to rest, but I wondered if it was ever used for naughty kids to come and sit because they had messed up in the classroom. Little did I know that question would be surprisingly and deservedly answered in only a few months.

Mom unlocked the padlock on the door. Marie Roberts, a longstanding family friend and a school board member, had brought the key by our place the day before. (Marie was the daughter-in-law of old Bob Roberts, who I have previously written about, and mother of Kenneth and Glenn who would be in my class this year.)

In the classroom, the first thing to grab my attention

was a big potbelly woodstove in the middle of the room. Hmmm. Who gets the wood? Who starts the fire on cold mornings? Who keeps the fire going during the school day? Does the school custodian take care of these things?

Other than the stove, many other things in the classroom seemed to fit. The row of desks with the same fancy wrought-iron footings that we had in Denair were hooked together in rows, but they looked very old and some were very small. Oh, that's right, all the grades were in one room so there would be some little people here.

The chalkboards, the roll-down maps, the windows on one side of the room, the American flag and pictures of two well-known presidents displayed in the front of the room—all were familiar. The oiled wood floor was something different, as was the little sectioned off area in the back of the room that served as a kitchen.

Mom told us that a cook would come in every day and prepare lunch for the Indian kids. I wondered if my heritage could be adjusted during the noon hour so I also could eat those lunches.

Over the next several weeks, Mom spent more time going to the school to get things ready for the September opening. Bette and I, eager to get more familiar with our new classroom and to help our mom prepare, often went with her.

We learned to use the Hecktograph to make copies of schoolwork for the kids. Mom would make a master using the special indelible pencil, and then we would take one sheet of paper at a time, place it on the gelatin pad, and give it a gentle rub to make a copy.

Bette and I were eager for school to start and yet we

were somewhat apprehensive. While we were sweeping floors, cleaning chalkboards, washing windows and dusting desks, we also thought about this curiosity: I had red hair and Bette was a towhead, while the rest of the students were dark-haired Indians.

Mom assured us this would not be a major problem since they were just kids like us. Okay for now, but we'll see how it goes on the first day of school.

About a week before school started, two Indian boys came to our house (the hotel) and introduced themselves as Warren and Billy Abbott. They lived across the river and a couple of miles downriver from the bridge. They had heard about the new teacher and her family, and came to get acquainted and to offer some helpful information.

Warren was going to be a sophomore at Hoopa High School, the same as my brother Mark, and said both boys could get a ride each morning to Weitchpec with the local mailman, Neil McKinnon. At Weitchpec, they could catch the school bus to Hoopa. It was a big problem solved.

Billy would be a seventh grader at our school like me and he was pretty sure there weren't any eighth graders that year. He said that meant he and I would have some special duties at the school that we could discuss later.

I liked Billy right off. He wasn't pushy, and it seemed like he really wanted to be helpful. Both of these guys were impressive, open and friendly, and Mark and I enjoyed having a heads-up and a good friend as we began the year in our Indian schools.

On the first day of school, Bette and I went early with

Mom to help make sure everything was ready for the kids. The weather was still warm, so there was no need to fire up the stove.

Oh, there was no custodian, and yes, you guessed it, Mom would be the fire-maker on chilly days, and it looked like a whole bunch of us would be sweeping the floors and emptying the wastebaskets.

The kids began arriving, some coming down the trail from their homes up on the mountain, some coming up the road from downriver. Billy Abbott and his two younger brothers came from their home across the river and down the road that ran by the hotel.

My presence and Bette's as the new kids in school seemed to be of minor concern, as the rest of them were more interested in chatting with each other and finding out about the news of their summer activities.

And they all wore regular clothes, like Bette and I did. Nobody was barefoot; there were no moccasins or deerskin shirts. Other than the fact that they all had dark hair and only slightly darker skin than most of my former fellow students, this whole scene could have happened in Denair.

They were kids—plain old everyday American kids. This might work out pretty well.

Chapter 28

The Rise and Fall of Social Titans

Billy Abbott, my seventh grade Indian buddy, and I were the "big kids" in Martin's Ferry School. Big is always a relative term, but we considered our qualifications obvious justification for the title.

There were no eighth graders in the school that year, and Billy and I were the only seventh graders—clear and compelling logic that placed us at the very top of the school's social structure, even if that structure was the shaky assemblage of only 22 other students in grades one through six.

That was a brand new status for each of us, and only our social naiveté kept the dark seeds of pomposity from finding fertile ground. Last year we were just sixth graders—no bragging rights there—and besides, this was my first year at the school, so there was no record of amazing achievements or even tawdry tales of transgressions. Gingerly, we were beginning to feel our way along this unfamiliar path of responsibility to others, and it was beginning to feel good.

Billy had told me of the specific and traditional responsibilities for the big kids of the school, almost like a historical mandate. Billy and I were now the ones to carry it on and to assume the mantle of importance.

Major big task number one: Keep the wood box in the classroom supplied with wood from the outside woodshed—kindling and various sizes of wood. A local Indian was annually contracted to keep the outside woodshed supplied with at least two cords of split oak and pine, but Billy and I were responsible for getting that wood inside for 1) the hungry potbellied stove in the middle of the classroom producing warmth and comfort (and humidity from the ever present teakettle on top of the stove) on winter days, and 2) the cook stove in the small kitchen where Alice, an Indian lady from up the hill, came in every day to prepare hot lunches for the whole school of 24 kids, including the minority white student population.

These were the uncontracted but clearly understood responsibilities of the school's big kids. To Billy and me, that looked like "Don't let them kids freeze or starve" duties. This was serious stuff, and we were hide-bound to prove our budding manhood or at least show that we could handle what was expected.

Major big kid task number two: Keep the school's water system working. When the school's only water faucet in the kitchen didn't produce, you might think an immediate call went out to the city water department. Only there wasn't any city and certainly no water department. Instead, you guessed it, the "big kids" were called in.

"Billy and Paul, we need some help!" We were told

of the problem and off we hustled up the hill behind the school to the creek where the school water tank was located to fix the problem. Often, especially after a storm, leaves and other debris clogged the penstock that channeled the water from the creek to the water tank.

Once we had the water flowing again, it was back down to the school to clean the mud off our shoes and get back to classroom activities. We had no complaints. Out of school, hiking up a muddy trail *doing a man's job*—we loved every bit of it.

Billy and I were just beginning to enjoy our high-ranking status and were expecting the rest of the kids to grant us at least some measure of respect. They were actually coming along well until one fine December morning. Oh, what a day! There are times in our jaunty stroll along life's pathway when circumstances intervene, when self-adulation seems to morph from fantasy into something else in life's stark reality. This was such a day.

The disaster that overtook Billy and me went far beyond merely putting a dent in our imagined polished image—it smashed it to smithereens.

After this day, every kid in Martin's Ferry School could easily identify with us as mere mortals, or more accurately, as just "one of us kids." The truth-revealing details are reluctantly disclosed in the next story.

Chapter 29

Billy and Me and the Skunk

That year at Martin's Ferry was my first real experience at primitive mountain living. My adjustment to this new way of life was coming along quite well, and it received a major boost as my Indian pal, Billy, took on the challenge of introducing me to some of the traditional ways of the locals.

As winter was coming on, it was natural that one of the early adventures was trapping, as in setting a trap, catching an animal, skinning it and drying the hide, and hopefully selling that fur for real money.

My reading adventures in the previous years had included the wild exploits of the Mountain Men in the early to mid 1800s, trapping beavers throughout the western mountains. They would pack out loads of pelts (called plews) after a winter in the bush and sell them to an agent of the Hudson Bay Company, Astor's Pacific Fur Company or the Northwest Fur Company. That was a little beyond my reach, but you have to start somewhere.

Billy had helped me skin the first raccoon I caught, but dressing out my second one was up to me. It mostly went well until attempting to peel the tail. I jerked too hard instead of a slow and steady pull, and off came the whole tail, not just the skin.

"Small matter," you say, "it's only the tail." Oh, no. This was no small matter since the raccoon's beautifully ringed tail is one of its distinctive identifying features along with the bandit-like masked eyes. Can you imagine Davy Crockett (*"Born on a mountaintop in Tennessee ..."*) donning a coonskin cap without a tail? Or when your parents bought that coonskin cap at Disneyland and it had no tail? Not good. Not good at all. The skin was ruined and a tough lesson learned.

Then came that fateful morning when checking my traps on the way to school, I found a skunk caught in one of my traps. Whoa, Nellie! I was not ready for this. I needed help, a level of expertise far beyond mine. I quickly left the skunk and hustled down the old Indian trail that led to the road the Abbott boys took on their way to school.

I had to catch Billy and snatch him for some desperately needed assistance before they got past. What luck! I saw the boys down the road below me. "Hey, Billy!" I called. "I need some help. I've got a skunk in my trap."

Billy sent his brothers on to school and we made our way back up the trail to the scene of my capture, a small swale just off the trail beside a little brook. Billy took a look and informed me I had not caught a skunk skunk, but a Spotted Skunk, which is slightly smaller than the more prolific Striped Skunk.

It had delicate black and white markings and a more valuable pelt, but it was still a skunk.

Education lesson delivered, we went to work on the skinning process with my faithful instructor taking the lead. I did not object. Billy casually mentioned that the most critical concern in skinning a skunk is to avoid puncturing the scent gland. That seemed logical enough, so okay, we would be careful. But in my newness to this wildlife world, I did not comprehend the potential gravity of such an error.

I was thankful to have a wilderness friend in times like these, one skilled in the fine art of skinning a skunk. We were nearing the end of our careful maneuvers with our knives when IT HAPPENED!!! It became immediately and odiferously obvious that the tragic mistake had been made. There were no second chances. There were no "do overs." There were no debates of who did what or why. This was the real thing. The dirty deed had been done and it called for action right now.

The scene suddenly changed from two stalwart young would-be mountain men carrying out age-old customs of their forbearers—his much more likely than mine—to a couple of frantic kids in one fine mess. Fighting the nauseating smell, we made short work of closing down operations and dashed to the creek to do whatever we could to staunch the stench that had so suddenly overtaken our small forest world.

The delicate beauty of Maiden Hair Fern and the warm, friendly scents of the woodland's vegetation in a moment lost their charm to the overpowering presence of skunk. We vigorously splashed. We scrubbed and rubbed as we made what we desperately hoped would be progress toward becoming somewhat acceptable, but soapless cold water has its limitations.

This was still a school day. Play hooky? Skip school

altogether? Never crossed our minds. We went off to school. Maybe they wouldn't notice—did we have a prayer? No, I think God has a sense of humor.

We arrived a little late, the reason for our delay likely having been shared by Billy's brothers. We had no sooner stepped across the threshold of the classroom door when any and all doubt about the reason for our tardiness vanished, like someone blew out the coal oil lamp. Kenneth, a knowing and aware fifth grader, summed it up succinctly: "Them boys got their selves a skunk. Get out of here! Whooee!!"

We were promptly banished—there was no need for a trial or a plea or even any discussion—to the outside porch where we did our work for the rest of the day. We sat on the porch bench with boxes for desks, much to our chagrin, and obviously to the amusement of the rest of the kids, as evidenced by the furtive glances and poorly-cloaked grins as they passed by on their way out to recess.

I'm sure some of the stories told to parents that evening included, "The teacher didn't put up with any nonsense from the big kids," "Billy and the teacher's kid got theirs today," and without question, "Boy, did they stink!"

Are there any lessons to be learned from this tale? Right off the top would be don't try skinning a skunk on a school day, or a reminder of the old adage, "Into every life a little rain (or a deluge) must fall," or even "Pride goeth before a fall." In this case, that translates to, "The big kids' shenanigans and semi-skilled surgical hands goeth before porch banishment, total embarrassment, and a return to the real world for two adventuresome and very human seventh grade boys."

A history altering event? Hardly. A vivid memory-producing happening? Unquestionably for me, and bringing a smile to my face as I write, and hopefully to yours as well.

I also suspect that floating into your frontal lobes are a few, or many, hazy or bold memories of hijinks or unusual happenings of your own, possibly bringing smiles or chuckles to you—to be shared with others—or maybe not.

Chapter 30

A Christmas Bear

That first Christmas, when my dad was in Blue Lake serving as an interim pastor with my sister, Mary, helping him, and my oldest brother, Ben, was in southern California at a Bible college, Mom, my older brother Mark, my younger sister Bette and I were still living in the hotel in Martin's Ferry. We four were adjusting to our new lifestyle, with no electricity and no indoor plumbing.

We were learning a little bit of what it means to live off the land. We had been given salmon from the Klamath River and deer meat, one of the staples of the sparse population in the area, and we had enjoyed the bounty of huckleberries and blackberries in pies and pancakes.

But the next chapter in our initiation to life with the Yurok Indians was totally unexpected and proved to be a most memorable experience.

One Saturday morning in December, our landlady, Annie Jacobs, got a call from John Luddington with the announcement that he had shot a bear the day before and had some bear meat for the Jennings clan.

Bette and Mark would be going to live in Blue Lake during the Christmas vacation, but at that time were still with Mom and me, so we three kids set off on the two mile hike up the steep twisting mountain road to John Luddington's place at the end of the road.

The dusting of snow we'd had the night before became more substantial as we trudged up the mountain. The clouds had burned off, and while it was still cold, the day was bright and sunny. We chatted about our rare fortune to be able to meet John Luddington, the almost mysterious Mountain Man, to see where and how he lived and to accept his unusual offer.

We arrived at the Luddington place and were immediately treated to an unforgettable scene. The neat weathered ranch house was nestled in the center of a large clearing of several acres. The ground up here was covered with two to three inches of snow. A small barn stood behind the house, and in the corral were five or six horses.

As breathtaking as was the entire scene, our attention was drawn to a large apple tree in front of the house from which hung the dressed carcass of a bear. The white fat on the body of the bear glistened in the frosty morning sunlight. The hide was draped over a stack of wood, and the dark, grizzled head and paws rested on an old stump.

We stopped and just stared in amazement at what we were seeing. Our feet crunching in the snow, our breath clouding in the chilly mountain air, a storybook view of the entire spread, and that bear! Had there been any doubt in our minds about the reputation of John Luddington as a hunter and trapper, it was promptly erased. This was real and that bear was real.

A couple of wary but almost friendly dogs had announced our arrival, and John and his lady came out of the house. Bette and I knew Alice, as she was the one who came down the hill to our school every morning and fixed lunch for all of the kids.

John Luddington even looked the part of a hunter/mountain man. He was well built, stocky, not tall, with a swarthy complexion, unshaven face, and he was wearing a black cowboy hat, a tanned leather vest and had a hunting knife attached to his belt.

His gruff appearance didn't seem to fit his gentleness as he greeted us and then he stepped forward and gave us a small sack. With a slight smile, he said, "I had some good luck hunting, and I thought your mom might like to fix some bear meat for you."

I'm sure we offered our thanks, or at least I think Mark did because I was too taken with that large bear hanging from the tree. I had a zillion questions I wanted to ask. How did he get the bear? I looked at the head and paws on the stump and I almost shuddered being this close to the white teeth and the long, curved claws.

Had he been in any danger? Had he loaded it on one of his horses? Was the horse spooked by having the body of a bear on its back? How much did it weigh? But I was speechless.

John must've sensed my curiosity because he gave us a brief explanation. "I shot the bear yesterday morning just about a mile up the mountain from here. My dogs had been setting up a fuss the last few days, so I knew a bear was in the area. This is my first bear of the season." Then he asked, "Have you ever eaten bear meat?" I think he knew the answer to that question; we admitted this would be a first for us. He assured us we would enjoy it. Then after a short pause he added, "It's good for you."

I was still finding it hard to put all this together. There was John Luddington and there was Alice. In the corral were his horses, and there was his snug-looking house.

And there was that bear, that huge bear. It had to be huge because Indian hunters never killed a small bear. Maybe we should thank him, not just for the meat, but for taking a dangerous predator out of our neighborhood.

Reluctantly we said our goodbyes and turned and, after one glance back at the bear, started on our way back down the mountain, discussing the whole way the unusual event we had just experienced.

Little did I realize that about a month later, I would meet John Luddington again in a very different and challenging situation.

Mom was eager to hear our story and we were eager to tell it—the snow, the farmhouse, the apple tree and the bear. We were also eager to have a taste of our rare treat, and that evening we did. I don't remember how Mom prepared the meat, but I do remember the excitement of that first bite.

It might have been a little tough, but the flavor was distinctive and undoubtedly enhanced by my thinking that this was a part of the bear that just a couple days before was running wild in the forest not far from our home. This meat was from the bear that John Luddington shot. And it was good for us!

Mom kept the extra meat in our cooler out by the spring, and the following weekend, when we went to Blue Lake, the entire family enjoyed a bear dinner. It was still a little tough, but a tasty reminder of the reality of this new life in Indian country.

Chapter 31

John Luddington

Indian Mountain Man

It should have been a normal weekday morning as I made my way along the forest trail to the one-room Martin's Ferry school.

But nothing was normal anymore, not since we moved here six months ago from a rural town in the Central Valley of California.

There we had electric lights and indoor plumbing. We had only a few sidewalks, but we had paved roads.

We had not yet gone modern in the early 1940s with a new electric refrigerator, but we had a very nice icebox that accommodated a 25-pound of ice, which we replenished a couple of times a week when the iceman came with his ice truck. Keeping the meat and fruits and veggies cool was important to Mom and Dad; for us kids, the best part was getting a two-stick popsicle for a nickel from the friendly iceman.

Here in Martin's Ferry, as mentioned, there was no electricity or paved roads or running water. There were kerosene lamps and outhouses at our home in the hotel and at school. But over the past two years, I had unknowingly primed myself for this new kind of life by discovering and plunging into the horizon-expanding adventures of reading.

I sailed the wild seas and tasted the salt spray on my lips as a deckhand with Todd Moran in the Howard Pease sea stories. Jack London in *White Fang* led me into the frozen Yukon with his faithful dog, Buck.

I was friends with Silver Chief: Dog of the North, thanks to the book of that title by Jack O'Brien. I huddled on the raft with Huckleberry Finn and Jim. And now those former fantasies were taking on an exciting sense of reality.

The progress in adjusting to my new surroundings had been due in large part to my friendship with Billy Abbott. Of course, learning to trap through his instruction, notwithstanding the skunk debacle, had been important, but just being buddies was a tremendous boost.

Since Billy and his family lived across the river from the school, he and his younger brothers crossed it on the old Martin's Ferry suspension bridge every day on their way to school. I often joined them on the narrow dirt road just below my place and walked with them the half-mile to school.

After school we went out onto the bridge and sailed paper airplanes into the wind and did other things that boys like to do from high places (one soon learns to be aware of wind directions) while watching the mighty Klamath some hundred feet below wind its way to the Pacific Ocean. I was amazed as we saw huge Chinook salmon leaping in the river on their determined journey to their spawning grounds.

On the morning in question, I took a different route to school, as I did several times each week to check on the traps I'd set on the mountain above our house and along a small creek.

Douglas fir, tan oak and cedar trees dominated my forest domain with huckleberries and gooseberries providing tasty diversions. The moist coolness along the creek encouraged mossy rocks, maidenhair fern and trillium. Small wonder that my target quarry for that area were raccoons, skunks, fishers, and possibly mink and fox that would be attracted to this woodland wonder.

My excitement on these morning ventures was always tempered by the realization that there were also larger critters that called this forest home: black bears (as I had learned from John Luddington), wild hogs and even cougars, none of which I had a hankering to meet up close and personal.

The first part of my morning venture was normal, checking the traps, which that morning had yielded nothing. I carefully re-baited and reset the traps, using a Swamp Robin I had shot the evening before.

Billy called this quiet forest bird a Swamp Robin and that was good enough for me. I later learned from "The Sibley Field Guide to Birds" that Varied Thrush is the proper name. I also learned that securing baits for the traps was a natural and necessary part of trapping.

I scrambled up out of the creek area where my traps were and was hurrying on to school along the old Indian trail when I felt the urgent call of nature. I realized there would not be enough time for me to get to the privacy of the school's "two-holer" outhouse. And, as there was no issue of privacy here on the trail, I positioned myself appropriately on a branch, which hovered about a foot and a half off the ground.

And then, hold it! (Pardon the pun.) The cool morning stillness was no more. Someone or something was on the trail above me and coming in my direction.

Bear? Could be. There were still huckleberries on the bushes, and it was a known fact that bears like huckleberries. I hope he doesn't prefer white meat.

But wait, do I hear horses' hooves? Can't be! The only one beside me who might ever use this trail—oh, gosh no—not John Luddington!

My mind was frantically racing. John Luddington: Indian hunter, trapper, loner, a fair man but reportedly not one to be trifled with.

John Luddington—Army veteran, expert with guns, a big man with a swarthy complexion, black mustache and in my mind a real mountain man—was indeed coming down the trail.

I had met him only once, about six weeks before, when Mark, Bette and I had hiked up the mountain to his ranch to pick up some bear meat for our family.

But there were a bunch of us together at that time; now it was only him and me. I secretly admired him, but at the same time feared him.

It would be good to meet him again, but certainly not this way, not with my pants down. Oh, this was not good.

It really was him. I first saw his weathered black Stetson appear above the rise on the trail, not more than 25 yards away, and then the man himself, astride his black stallion and leading a pack horse. The clanging of some traps, dangling from the gear on the pack horse, mingled with the squeaks of the leather of John's saddle. One of the horses blew.

My choices of action were obviously very limited. Hide behind the tree? Nope, too late for that.

Assume the confident demeanor of a fellow outdoorsman? Hard to do with shaking knees and a cotton mouth. I did my very hasty and awkward best to return to a reasonable state of respectability—pants up, belt buckled, shirt tucked.

John continued down the trail and drew up his horse not 10 feet from me. He knew who I was from our one brief meeting at his place.

I wanted to meet him as one mountain man to another, but for some reason, that fantasy didn't fit my current predicament.

John gave me a quizzical and somewhat surprised look. I think he said, "Good morning" and asked how I was doing that day.

With as much poise and confidence I could muster, I stammered, "I'm checking my traps."

"Any luck?" he asked. When I told him that I had not, he confessed that it was sometimes the same with him, although I doubted that. I think he wished me a good day. He nodded to me, gave his horse a gentle knee, and moved on down the trail. I knew he trapped across the river along Pine Creek.

I stared in wonder and relief. Wow! I had just met and survived a close one-on-one encounter with big John Luddington.

What was he thinking about that skinny white kid who thought he knew how to trap? What would he tell

Alice about our meeting? My questions seemed to be answered a couple of days later when Alice quietly told me that big John would like to take me with him to run his trap lines on Saturday if I would like to go.

Oh, brother, would I ever!

Chapter 32

A Day to Remember ... Or Forget

Saturday morning came, trapping day with John Luddington, and what should have been a momentous day of unforgettable experiences was not to be.

It wasn't that John Luddington had decided against our outing. It certainly wasn't that I had chickened out. Other plans from higher authorities had taken over and another lesson reluctantly learned.

My mother had made arrangements with our close friends, the Roberts, to keep their son, Kenneth, a good schoolmate of mine, with us for the day while they went to town. On any other weekend, this would have been a welcome event, but John Luddington ...

Early Saturday morning we heard the horses down below the house. Mom went out on the back steps and told John that something had come up and I was not able to go with him that day. John nodded and started on with his horses.

A few minutes later I heard the horses' hooves on the

wooden decking of the Martin's Ferry bridge as John made his way across the river to Pine Creek and his trapping. I watched John on his big black horse, his packhorse trailing behind, with another saddled horse also trailing. Its saddle was empty.

I'm sure Kenneth and I had fun playing that day. But part of the time I wondered about what it would have been like.

Would John have brought lunch, or did he go all day without eating? Maybe he'd have some smoked salmon or venison jerky, or maybe Alice had made him cookies or sandwiches. What would he have talked about? How many animals had he trapped that year and what kind? How much would I have learned about setting a trap that was different from what I learned from Billy?

Many questions with no answers, only the thoughts or fantasies of what might have been.

Some of the fear of John Luddington is gone. The awe and respect remain strong, all these years later.

Chapter 33

Scalping Woodpeckers

My eagerness to soak up this pioneer living/Indian culture was aided and abetted by old "Mr. Jim," an elderly Indian gentleman who came by occasionally to visit Annie Jacobs, our landlady, at our Martin's Ferry Hotel home.

Mr. Jim, unlike many of the other aged Indians, was easy to talk with and always ready to share something about his Indian culture. I was intrigued by this visitor who had so much to offer, and I think he was just as intrigued by this eager-to-learn young white lad.

During our chats, usually as we sat on a rickety old bench out in the yard, he taught me several Indian phrases. My favorite was "te' e' noich" (please employ a pronounced glottal stop and a soft K sound), meaning "It's hot!"

Mr. Jim thought this would be a very practical term to use and I readily agreed, so I tried it out many times on my Indian friends over the next couple of years.

The responses were consistently blank stares. I've

chalked up the problem to be the differences in the several acknowledged dialects of the Indians along the river. Or could it possibly be my pronunciation of the term? Nah, couldn't be that.

Now, many years later when feeling the effects of a particularly hot day, I will voice that rare expression apparently known to only a few native language linguists —Mr. Jim and me—"te' e' noich." And the memories that come flooding back of Mr. Jim on that rickety old bench and woodpecker scalps are invariably accompanied by a cooling, soothing breeze.

Woodpecker scalps? Yes. Mr. Jim offered to increase my economic standing by paying for woodpecker scalps. You heard that right—the scalp of a woodpecker, and it was worth money.

I was at first dumbfounded as this was a completely foreign concept to me, as I suspect it is to you as you are reading this. He said some of his friends were repairing old Indian headdresses and that the brightly colored woodpecker scalps had long been an integral part of those items, often requiring as many as 75 to 100 woodpecker scalps for one ceremonial headdress. The headdresses are part of the regalia worn in some of their traditional dances.

When he was leaving that day, after sharing this unbelievable idea with me, he said he would be back in several days, and if I had a woodpecker at that time, he would show me how to properly scalp it.

This presented an interesting dilemma. Billy Abbott had shown me the necessity of killing birds to use for bait in my traps, and I had accepted that. Now an ancient tradition of decorating ceremonial headdresses with woodpecker scalps could be delayed if not enough scalps could be found. And Mr. Jim had suggested a way that I could help.

Wow! And he would pay me a whopping 10 cents for the scalp of a small woodpecker, an Acorn or Downy Woodpecker, and an amazing 25 cents for the scalp of a large woodpecker, a hard-to-find Pileated Woodpecker, the largest woodpecker in North America.

Sure enough, three or four days later Mr. Jim was back, and I was ready with my first Acorn Woodpecker kill, and the scalping lesson began.

Under his very careful supervision, I made the cut from the bill, including the top half of the bill, around the back of the bird's head so that all of the critical red feathers were included. Then taking hold of the top half of the bill, I gently but firmly peeled back the scalp, and there it was—a real woodpecker's scalp.

The old gentleman told me I had done a good job. I felt Indian blood coursing through my veins. My sixth grade buddies back in Denair would never believe what I had just done. I could hardly believe it myself.

We flattened the scalp out on a board to dry it, and on Mr. Jim's next visit, he took the scalp, and my retirement fund was enriched by one shiny dime. My business/hunting adventure probably produced a total of a half dozen of small woodpecker scalps. The prized Pileated Woodpecker was too elusive for this young marksman.

On several occasions over the years, I have seen the Indian headdresses with the woodpecker scalp adornments in museums and visitor centers, and I wondered if any of those scalps had been supplied by an enterprising white chap from Martin's Ferry.

While I will never know if my unusual handiwork is anywhere on display, I will always know the feeling of pride I had in being part of a centuries-old cultural tradition of the Klamath River Indians.

Chapter 34

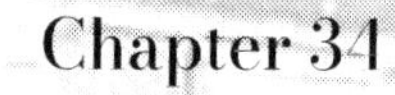

Special Saturday Adventures

We had been following old game trails most of the morning, and the one we were on now showed encouraging signs of recent activity.

Suddenly Billy stopped and raised his hand.

We both froze, listening to the rustling in the brush up ahead of us.

Moments later a forked horn came into view, not 30 yards away, and stopped when he saw us. We both brought up our rifles, took quick aim and fired. The deer took a few faltering steps and dropped.

"Oh, boy, we got him!" Billy's excitement betrayed his usually calm demeanor. We approached the deer slowly and found there was no more movement.

I had spent the previous night at Billy's, and at first light we were on our way up to the ridge above his place. This hunting experience was a first for me, but Billy had gone on many hunts with his dad and his older brother.

This was his first time as the top guy with a hunting partner.

The process of getting the deer ready to be moved was overwhelming to me. Field dressing a deer was a whole lot different than taking care of a raccoon that I had trapped or fixing a chicken for Sunday dinner. Once again Billy's experience was called on and proved to be effective because there's a whole lot of blood and guts in a deer.

He was mighty glad that it was a small deer and not a big 4-pointer, which would've posed a serious transportation problem. While I picked up our two rifles and the deer's head, Billy hoisted the carcass onto his shoulders and we were off. Fortunately our homeward trek was only about two miles and mostly downhill.

I was happy to accept the congratulations that came our way from Mr. Abbott. Without any need to make a comment, all of us understood that this was Billy's hunt and he had done it well. I was also happy to accept the sandwich that Mrs. Abbott made for me to enjoy on my way back to my hotel home. The deer meat that Mom and I enjoyed later in the week was outstandingly delicious.

This hunting venture had taken place on one of those Saturdays when Dad had taken Mom to Blue Lake for the weekend, and I had elected to stay in Martin's Ferry to not only enjoy Annie Jacob's cooking, but also the opportunity to explore the wilderness country on the mountain above our place. This was not a regular occurrence because my folks knew that a closer brush with civilization for me on the Blue Lake weekends was not to be totally ignored.

The normal routine for my lone explorations would be that after breakfast with Annie and fortified with the sandwich she would have made, I'd take my .22 and follow a couple of old sled roads up the mountain and just wandered through the prairies and timbered areas.

Hunting or shooting never seemed to be the priority for these adventures, but merely having a gun and exploring alone in uninhabited country, I had no trouble identifying with famous frontiersmen of our country's past. I was Daniel Boone and Kit Carson, but I was also thankful not to have to swim swollen rivers or hide from unfriendly natives.

On one occasion, I came across what appeared to be an old dilapidated sawmill, which Annie told me was probably used to cut lumber for building the hotel 100 years before. I also found traces of a well-known but now abandoned trail leading to Weitchpec. This had been the main route for the downriver and coastal Indians before the road was put in, also nearly 100 years before. ...

While I was there on the mountain I got out my crosscut saw, felled a Douglas fir and dragged it to the sawmill. And I hauled that lumber down the mountain and nailed the boards, using square nails, on the walls of the new hotel. I also trudged along the trail with some other Indians carrying abalone shells and dried surf fish from the coast to exchange with the upriver tribes for acorns and a couple of fox pelts ...

Time to end my daydreaming. Maybe I'll just head back down the hill and see if Annie has supper ready.

One other memorable and telling incident occurred on my mountain wanderings. At the edge of a clearing one rainy morning I came upon a huge hawk perched in a gnarled oak tree. The "hunter" in me said, "Rare target; what a great opportunity!" I quickly brought the .22 to my shoulder, put the sights on the majestic bird *and I could not pull the trigger*.

I remember wondering why this had happened. I was not sorry it did. And I was glad that hawk was still free to fly the skies above Martin's Ferry.

I also reflected on killing Swamp Robins and other small birds to bait my traps and shooting woodpeckers to provide scalps for Indian headdresses. And while that seemed justified because each was an accepted practice among the Indians, there would never be justification for the result of the fiasco in Denair with my slingshot and the Cedar Waxwing.

In two weeks I'll go to Blue Lake with Mom and Dad for the weekend and enjoy time with the family.

On Sunday we'll go to church and sing, "A Shelter in the Time of Storm" and "Trust and Obey," and I'll be reminded that life's lessons are not limited to tromping alone through the wilderness.

Chapter 35

My Pugilistic Beginnings and Endings

There was a long list of firsts in my seventh grade year at Martin's Ferry School. Most of them centered around being in a one-room school with Yurok Indian classmates and living a pioneer lifestyle.

The Indian kids were not nearly as impressed with the new white kid as the new white kid was with the Indian kids.

In the classroom, the teacher—my mom—created an easy, friendly atmosphere, and at the same time, we realized there were times when we had to buckle down and tend to math and writing and history.

On the playground we played dodge ball and Red Rover and kickball, as did kids everywhere. But the kids in Denair did not have a hillside next to the playground that featured tan oak trees, which produced a carpet of leaves that made for easy sledding.

That's sledding, as in sitting on a piece of cardboard and letting gravity take its course. I don't recall anyone going airborne, but it made for one exciting trip down the hill to a sometimes hard landing at the playground. A couple of boys brought some wooden sleds they had made, and they came even closer to breaking the sound barrier on the race down the hill.

Another first, even more memorable than downhill racing on tan oak leaves, came early in the school year when Dutchy Mitchell asked me one day if I would like to learn how to box. I already knew his older brother was active in the boxing circles in Eureka, and now Dutchy informed me that his brother had taught him how to box and he would like to share some of that knowledge.

Understand that Dutchy, though a sixth grader, was well put together and outweighed me by probably 10, maybe 15 pounds. During that seventh grade year, I recall the proud moment when the school scales showed I had reached a strapping 100 pounds.

Dutchy brought some boxing gloves to school and we agreed that after school that day, we would have our boxing lesson. I was eager to learn but also apprehensive about our session. Dutchy knew boxing, while I had never even put my hand into a boxing glove.

But my fears were mostly put aside because Dutchy, in an honest and almost gentlemanly manner, taught me some of the rudiments of boxing. There was the stance, position of the feet, holding the gloves in a defensive position, throwing a punch, blocking a punch, and so much more.

Over the next couple of weeks, Dutchy and I put on the gloves probably half a dozen times, eventually sparring effectively, each of us landing some respectable blows, but at no time did my young Yurok boxing instructor take advantage of his superior size or skills. I was thankful, and the respect we had for each other and our friendship grew stronger.

My newly acquired boxing skills were put to the test the following year in Blue Lake Elementary School, where as an eighth grader, I again was one of the big kids, this time with Arnold Davis, also an Indian.

Boxing seemed to be a big thing at the school and it was not unusual during the noon hour to see boys from the fourth grade on up donning boxing gloves and going at it. Eventually the pressure was on to see the big boys—Arnold and me—square off.

One noon hour Arnold and I did go one drawn-out round, but those hoping to see a bruising, bloody battle were sorely disappointed. Neither Arnold nor I were possessed with a killer instinct when it came to boxing.

We probably put on a pretty good show, each landing some solid blows, and judging from the kids' yells, it might've been a championship bout. Arnold would probably have been declared the winner if a decision had been rendered. Neither of us asked for a rematch.

The lasting lesson for me in each of these boxing experiences was that both Dutchy and Arnold were Indians, but that seemed to have no effect on our activities.

We were friends and we were willing to pit our respective boxing skills against the other without anger or a need to prove anything other than our willingness to compete.

Chapter 36

Eeling on the Mad River

An Evening to Remember

At the end of my seventh grade year in Martin's Ferry, Mom and I left the reservation and joined the rest of the family in Blue Lake.

While Mom taught at a small school a couple of miles out of town, I was in the eighth grade at the Blue Lake Grammar School. We had three teachers there. The sixth, seventh and eighth grades were together, so Bette and I were classmates once again.

One of my eighth grade classmates was Arnold Davis, a Yurok Indian, whose older brother, Reggie, had become friends with my brother Mark the previous year as they rode the school bus together to Arcata High School.

That fall, Mark and I were invited by Reggie and Arnold, to join their family for a night of eeling (catching eels) on the Mad River. This was a major social event for the extended Davis family that was enjoyed several times a year when the eels were running. Mr. and Mrs. Davis agreed that it would be a good idea for those Jennings boys "to see how we did it." You bet, Mark and I won't pass up a chance to be part of this celebration.

Along toward evening a group of 15 to 20 Yurok revelers, family and friends, in-laws and possibly a few outlaws, and a couple of light-skinned visitors, all gathered around a huge bonfire a comfortable distance from the river's edge, enjoying the companionship of old and young. Arnold introduced me to his folks and some of his other relatives.

As darkness approached a number of young men prepared for the fishing part of the evening. Each equipped himself with a light, flashlight or lantern, and a short pole to which was attached a hook to snag the eels.

Eels are sucker fish that attach themselves to rocks on the bottom of the river and then move from rock to rock. They tend to be nocturnal with their moving upstream. When the eager eeler locates his prey in the light, a quick downward swipe with his pole snares the unfortunate eel and it is quickly transported to the shore to the waiting cooking committee—the women and older folks who no longer wish to scramble over the slippery rocks in the river.

I was fascinated by the way the eels were then carefully cleaned and cut into three inch pieces and tossed into the campfire coals. After an appropriate time for a goodly number of eels to be caught and for the eel pieces to be cooked, a fishing recess was called. The men came in from the river and warmed up by the fire.

The chunks of the eel were taken from the coals, the ashes and skin peeled off and the tasty white morsels were wrapped in pieces of freshly baked bread. I don't remember seeing any ketchup or mustard or mayonnaise. I just remember Mrs. Davis, my friend Arnold's mom, handing me my first ever eel sandwich.

I was going to say that I bravely chomped down on my sandwich, but since everyone around me was enjoying theirs—little kids, old men, even Mark and Reggie were halfway through their sandwich—this had nothing to do with bravery. It was more like, "You said you wanted to get into this Indian culture, so put your money where your mouth is." Or, more appropriately, put your mouth where your eel sandwich is.

Which I did, and the distinctive flavor didn't taste like chicken, which would have been enough by itself to make this a most delightful experience, but the entire scene—the campfire, surrounded by friendly and accepting Indians, and for the moment I was one of them—only added to the delicious eel sandwich. "Yes, please, I would like another."

This process was repeated several times during the evening until everyone's hunger had been delightfully assuaged and an ample supply of fire-roasted eel was put aside to be enjoyed another day. It was late when the party and fire finally wound down and folks headed for their homes. A good time had been had by all, but none more than by Mark and me, two white guests who had been introduced to another Yurok tradition. What an honor to be part of the festivities—another lasting memory created.

Cultural note: The Indians living on the Klamath River employed two other methods of fishing for eels. At the mouth of the river the men waded into the breakers for the eels that were starting their journey upstream to spawn, and used homemade hooks to snag the eels. Upriver where I lived, I recall the hand-woven baskets with a funnel opening on one end which, when anchored near the shore, trapped the eels.

I'm sure there is a reliable body of research that supports the thesis that a young man in his formative years, having ingested bear meat supplied by Indians (my hero John Luddington), venison from two stalwart young hunters, and savored the scrumptious slices of eel meat supplied by Indians (the Davis family), whale steaks that were available briefly during World War II, and having eaten either fresh rattlesnake or had been nearly eaten by a fresh rattlesnake (remember Pecwan) will experience a realignment of his DNA, prompting a predisposition to a lifelong enjoyment of Native American people and their culture and an ongoing yen for wilderness exploration.

Chapter 37

Out of the Past

I was eagerly looking forward to meeting with a small group of Native American members of the Hupa and Yurok tribes on the Hoopa Indian Reservation in the Klamath Mountains of northern California. (Hupa was the tribe's name; Hoopa was the name of their reservation).

I was there to gather some background information on two Indian men who had made a lasting impression on me years ago as a youngster living on the reservation. I wanted the stories of these two tribal elders to be accurate and bring honor to their memories. Bonny and Glenn Roberts were part of the family my folks had been close to over the years, and they had arranged for lunch at the Tribal Senior Center to kick-start my investigation.

We were just getting seated at the table when I noticed that the conversation stopped and all eyes were focused on the gentleman who had approached our table and was standing next to my chair. Bonny asked, "Paul, do you remember Buddy Bear?"

Buddy Bear? Yes, Buddy Bear was in the first grade and I was in the seventh grade in our one-room school 76 years ago. I welcomed the surprise of Buddy's appearance, but as I stood and shook hands with him, I struggled to connect this friendly gentleman with the first grader I had known.

Fortunately, an amusing and telling incident came to mind that occurred in our Martin's Ferry School so many years ago, and I took advantage of the situation and shared it with our group, much to Buddy's delight.

In our school, the older kids were regularly cast in the role of the teacher's helper to assist the younger kids with their schoolwork. Buddy and his twin sister, Tissy (real names Martin and Marcia) were a diminutive but dynamic duo. They were full of—well, they were full of life and a handful for the teacher, my mom. They even presented a challenge to whoever drew the short straw and was assigned to serve as the first grade helper that day. These little rascals were wired.

One fine fall morning, Buddy arrived at school with a big brightly colored bouquet for the teacher. (I saw a twinkle in Buddy's eyes). This touching gesture by our little scamp was a jolt for all of us.

My mom thanked Buddy profusely and congratulated him on his thoughtfulness. (I noticed Buddy was enjoying this.) Then she gently suggested that he take the colorful arrangement and lay it on the hillside next to the playground so that everyone could enjoy the colors at recess.

Buddy was now smiling broadly, but with feigned innocence, he interrupted: "I really didn't know that it was poison oak." The others at the table knew Buddy. They rolled their eyes and nodded knowingly. Buddy's feeble attempt to regain honest composure was weak at best. Still a rascal, and on this day a delightful interruption to my intended task.

The first of my character studies was John Luddington, of whom I have written previously. John had become a hero in my eyes while on the reservation. Having soaked up the adventures of our country's historical mountain men, I saw John Luddington as a present day, real life Mountain Man—hunting, fishing, trapping. He was also pretty much a loner—well-respected but apparently not a man to be trifled with. I imagined a Robin Hood-esque quality about John: "Feared by the bad, loved by the good. Robin Hood."[1]

The two times I had met John Luddington were both memorable. The first time was when Mark, Bette and I hiked up to his mountain home to accept his gift of bear meat that he had set aside for the new schoolteacher and her family. The image of a dressed carcass of a bear hanging from the apple tree in a snow-covered yard is not easily forgotten.

The other time was when on the trail to school one morning John Luddington surprised me while I was in a very compromising position. Life's most embarrassing moments have a way of annoyingly staying with us. Oh yes, I remember John Luddington.

Because of John's reclusive nature, my friends on that day at the Senior Center were hard-pressed to provide much that was new to me. But my fortune turned around the next day when I was put in touch with an old Indian friend of John's, somewhat of a mystery man himself.

I sensed some reluctance during my initial phone call to him, but he agreed to give me "a couple of minutes" later that day. I think my curiosity to learn more about John Luddington was matched by his curiosity to see what this old white guy was up to.

I met him in his small workshop. He continued to work on an Indian craft project, carving a bird from a buck horn, while we chatted. He was sharing some general things from John's life when he paused for a moment, put down his project, and quietly said, "John had supernatural powers, but I can't say much about that." Another pause, and a gaze out the open door out toward the hills. I knew enough not to push for details but my "Oh?" seemed enough to let him continue at his deliberate pace.

"Let me tell you a story about John." The old gentleman paused, as if considering whether he could share the story with me, then, looking directly at me, he continued. "When he was young, John and some of his friends went to Bluff Creek to have some booze. Liquor was illegal on the reservation back then."

I remember hearing of Bluff Creek as a remote hangout along the Klamath River.

"While they were drinking and just having some fun, a bear came out of the woods and attacked one of the kids. John quickly ran and jumped on the back of the bear. Holding onto the bear with one hand, he reached into his pocket and got out his knife. He opened the knife with his teeth and slit the bear's throat."

That was it, the end of the story. Was it supernatural power or uncommon bravery? Short, dramatic, apparently not widely known, and he suggested it would be best not to share where I heard the story. I wondered about the secrecy.

Did only a few people know about John's special ability? Would people tend to question whether it really happened? My hushed response was, "Wow! That's one heck of a story."

This prompted only a slight nod from my storyteller as if to say, "That's enough of a history lesson of John Luddington for today." And it was.

I thanked the old craftsman for his time and amazing information. He merely nodded in response and went back to his work on the carving project.

The other Indian gentleman from my past and on my short list that day was our mailman, Neil McKinnon. I was fortunate to arrange a meeting with Neil's granddaughter, DeeDee McKinnon. It was a delightful and informative time while she fleshed out some of the details of her grandfather's life.

In contrast to John Luddington, Neil was friendly, outgoing and willing to help others whenever he could, such as when he gave my brother Mark and his friend, Warren Abbott, a ride to Weitchpec so they could catch a bus to their high school.

Often on mornings when Neil was to pick up the boys, I would wait with them so I could have a brief chat with Neil about the weather or road conditions or the success of my trapping adventures—man-to-man stuff. He was always accommodating to me, I think sensing my eagerness to be part of this culture. We might not have solved many of the world's problems, but my world was definitely richer because of these short conversations with Neil. He always made it a good start to the day.

Neil's mail route was from the small community of Pecwan, which was 22 miles down the Klamath from our home in Martin's Ferry, and then upriver to Weitchpec. On his way over the twisting dirt road, he picked up the outgoing mail from the 50 or so families living along the river. He left his home near Pecwan every morning, gathering mail to be posted, picked up the high school kids who desperately wanted a ride, learned stories of the local happenings and deposited all of the same at the Weitchpec store/post office.

Those stories would be grist for the morning's discussion and debates by the local gentry who regularly gathered around the store's potbellied stove in cold weather or on the rickety wooden bench outside in warm weather.

But here is the winner: There was no other store along Neil's route, so this helpful, friendly and accommodating mailman *also gathered grocery/supply lists from his patrons* on his morning run and delivered those lists to the storekeeper at Weitchpec.

On the way back down the river in the afternoon, Neil delivered the mail, high school kids, latest news he had learned while palavering with other locals around the big woodstove in the middle of the store, and *he delivered the items from the supply list gathered that morning.*

Among some of the regular needs, there might be a bucket of lard, a bag of potatoes, a box of silk wicks for the lantern, some cans of evaporated milk (especially if the cow was dry), a bag of flour, a box of shells for a deer gun, and possibly an order from the Sears or Montgomery Ward catalogs.

Compensation for the special service? Nothing official, but perhaps a bag of apples, a Mason jar of put-up string beans, perhaps some salmon or a fresh cut of beef or venison, and if Neil's wife was under the weather, there could be a warm huckleberry pie. Seemed to work for everyone.

John Luddington and Neil McKinnon, two influential Indian men of my past, distinctly different, but each contributed in their own way to their communities. John helped friends and neighbors with building a house or with cattle round-ups. Neil was active in native cultural events and served as a "singer" for the Indian Brush Dance.

I am thankful for their significant contribution to my understanding and appreciation of life along the Klamath River, and for leaving me with a generous supply of beautiful and lasting memories.

Chapter 38

Closing Thoughts

Although decades have passed since my years living with the Indians and during the Depression years in rural California, I still feel that I was fortunate—no, blessed—to have crossed paths with such an unusual cast of characters and to have lived through such an improbable set of circumstances. The lessons learned have contributed to my wonderful treasure of memories that are still vivid to me, many of which I have shared with you.

As uniquely different as were the homes in which I lived, it was the adjustment to the abrupt change in the culture surrounding those homes that was the most challenging.

For instance, moving from primitive living in our log cabin in Pecwan when I was only 5 into a "normal" town provided more than a few of those "Good grief, what in the world is going on?" moments. There were many houses on many streets and many people all around. There were multiple rooms in our house, there were amazing stores right in town, and of course, there was indoor plumbing. In my short life, I hadn't had time to develop deeply ingrained habits, so adjusting to all of this newness came rather naturally to me, and for the most part, pleasantly.

During those next six years throughout grammar school, I formed a stronger understanding of myself and my world, this world with electric lights and running water, so that moving back to Martin's Ferry for my seventh grade year proved to be a dramatic and at times traumatic and exciting time in my life.

But consider some of the realities of that move. After the first few weeks, striking a match to light the lantern in the evening was fun. Then came the memory of flipping a switch, and behold, there was light. I remember taking a bath in the bathtub in Denair with warm water from faucet, but that was now only a memory as it was replaced by heating water on the stove and pouring it into a washtub.

Then there was the outhouse instead of a flush toilet. For you who hold romantic thoughts of a country outhouse, let me offer just a touch of reality. While in your private little house on a warm day, invariably there would be the presence of a friendly fly or an unfriendly bee, either of which might tickle you in your very tender places. Or on cold days, you soon learned a fresh meaning of "cold buns."

In Denair, I could scare up three or four guys to play flies and grounders almost anytime, but now the closest kid was more than a mile away. If we needed rolls for dinner in Denair, I could just run down to the store and pick some up. In Martin's Ferry, we'd have to just make do with some crackers.

My move to Martin's Ferry did pose many challenges, but I was much better prepared for them, even though they came about suddenly. My interest in pioneer and Old West times in our country and reading about those days had been a good primer for me. I could more easily accept turning back the cultural clock about 30 years to coal oil lamps and outhouses again. I did miss that indoor plumbing, though. But the one-room Indian school proved to be a rare and valuable learning experience.

I smile when I think of the people who were there at the right time and place in critical moments of my life. My motherly first grade teacher Mrs. DeLaMater lovingly helped bridge the gap from almost isolated living in Pecwan to an enjoyable school experience in Denair. The struggle of awkward goofy sixth graders to become more responsible adolescents seemed to require a cadre of behavioral specialists, and that describes my sixth grade teacher, Mr. Johnson. His patience, his understanding, his sense of humor and even his discipline helped provide an introduction to responsibility.

But more than that, it was the sense and understanding of respect that we learned from him—respect for ourselves and our classmates, adults and people who are different from us, and even the respect for what is right and just.

Not all of my "teachers" had teaching credentials. Harry Dillon, my independent sixth grade classmate, taught our whole class a stirring lesson of accepting responsibility when we screwed up. Through my seventh grade year with Billy Abbott, I learned that trust and friendship are a matter of character and not skin color. I also learned that skunks have a scent gland.

As with most of us, the influence of my family—immediate and/or extended—has had the greatest impact on my belief system and who I have become. The influence of my parents and their Christian faith obviously rings high in my overall learning and development. My siblings, especially Bette, 2 years younger than me, and Mark, two years older than me, were close during our growing up years, and I am thankful for their contributions to our fun times and our squabbles and our lasting friendship.

As I look back over this kaleidoscope of the early years of my life, I marvel at how those changing pieces—ordinary and a few extraordinary people, unusual events in disparate locations—blended together to give me a challenging, satisfying and memorable youth.

Was it just chance or circumstances? Were the joys and disappointments just part of the randomness of life?

No, I think a more rational explanation of this kaleidoscope has been the influence of some higher power. And that Higher Power, the Creator of the universe, gave us this promise through His prophet, Jeremiah:

"For I know the plans I have for you, plans to
prosper you and not harm you,
plans to give you hope and a future."
Jeremiah 29:11 (NIV)

I've had that hope and future for 90-plus years, and it is my hope that you may find the same in your own life.

You most likely didn't grow up living with Indian tribes or even in the Depression years, but I encourage you to look back over your own life and share stories of your history with your kids and grandkids.

And may you be richly blessed as you see the hand of God at work in your own life. It's the most fulfilling and amazing thing there is.

May God bless you.

Acknowledgments

I am so thankful for the many people who provided invaluable assistance in my venture to bring the story of my childhood to life.

Much of the verification of my Indian stories came from Hoopa residents, some of whom have been lifelong friends. Helen Roberts Pole researched early Humboldt County census records. Her brother, Glenn, and his capable wife, Bonnie, have contributed mightily regarding the memories of each of their families: the Roberts and the Marshalls. Janice Yerton, DeeDee McKinnon, Judy Surber and Byron Nelson have each added to my understanding of Native American life and mores, particularly of the Hupa, Yurok and Karuk people.

Jacquie Wincentsen offered valuable insights and prayer for my work. Mercie Marshall, my granddaughter and an outstanding young artist, drew the wonderful illustrations for the book. Author and literary agent Wendy Lawton was generous with her time and pointed me to the right people and path to take.

Huge thanks to the three people who have brought this book to completion and professional publication: Sue Nowicki, my expert editor, adviser and friend; Jerusha Agen, an amazing author herself who gave me wise advice and pulled the whole thing together into the finished project; and graphic designer and artist Kristen Ingebretson, who created the perfect cover for my book. What a pleasure to work with these three talented women!

Mere coincidence cannot explain the inspiration and encouragement I have felt through this whole process, nor the timely arrival of just the right people to provide needed assistance. I am very thankful for the faith that began so long ago in that rustic cabin in the woods, nourished by my parents and siblings. Thanks be to God.

Notes

20. Swimming and Watermelons

1. Mark Twain, *The Tragedy of Puddn'head Wilson* (1893)

22. Family Literary Lessons

1. Robert Lowry, "Christ Arose" (1874)
2. Lowry, "Christ Arose"

23. Before TV and Social Media, There Was Radio

1. Henry Wadsworth Longfellow, "Christmas Bells" (1863)

26. Martin's Ferry Hotel

1. The Humboldt Historian (July-August 1980)
2. Oscar Lord, "Pack Train Days in Humboldt County," in *The History of Humboldt County Schools*, ed. Evelyn McCombs Dieke (California: Pacific Lumber Company, 2003) 6:126.
3. The Humboldt Historian (March-April 1988)
4. The Humboldt Historian (March-April 1988)

37. Out of the Past

1. Carl Sigman, theme song from *The Adventures of Robin Hood* (United Kingdom, 1955)

About Paul Austin Jennings

Paul Austin Jennings was born in 1930 in the Indian hospital on the remote Hoopa Indian Reservation in Northern California where his parents were Christian missionaries.

After an unusual and exciting early life living among the Indians, and part of his grammar school years living during the Depression years in California's Central Valley, he went on to a successful 30-year career in education as a teacher, coach and administrator in both public and Christian schools. He holds California Lifetime Teaching and Administrative credentials.

The author's other ventures included serving as a licensed securities agent, conducting teacher training workshops across the country for a specialized reading program, and volunteering as a naturalist for the U.S. Fish and Wildlife service and in Oregon state parks.

In his earlier years, the author served in a Military Police unit of the California National Guard and operated a sports fishing concession on California's north coast.

The author's unique and varied experiences during his grammar school years have given him a keen insight in understanding the clashing and blending of different cultures. His writing reflects many of the major changes from the practices and beliefs of his generation to those of our present time, as well as the never-changing love from God.

Made in United States
Troutdale, OR
11/25/2024

25267742R00133